THE WORLD IN FLAMES

THE WORLD IN FLAMES

A Black Boyhood in a White Supremacist Doomsday Cult

JERALD WALKER

Beacon Press
Boston

BEACON PRESS
Boston, Massachusetts
www.beacon.org

Beacon Press books
are published under the auspices of
the Unitarian Universalist Association of Congregations.

19 18 17 16   8 7 6 5 4 3 2 1

This book is printed on acid-free paper that meets the uncoated paper
ANSI/NISO specifications for permanence as revised in 1992.

Text design and composition by Kim Arney

This is a true story. The names of many of the persons
mentioned, as well as some details and events surrounding
them, have been modified to protect their privacy.

A segment of this work originally appeared in
River Teeth as the essay "Captain Love."
Most Bible passages were quoted from the
English Standard Version.

Library of Congress Cataloging-in-Publication Data
Names: Walker, Jerald.
Title: The world in flames : a black boyhood in a white
supremacist doomsday cult / Jerald Walker.
Description: Boston : Beacon Press, 2016.
Identifiers: LCCN 2015034830 |
ISBN 9780807027509 (hardcover : alk. paper) |
ISBN 9780807027516 (ebook)
Subjects: LCSH: Walker, Jerald. | Worldwide Church of God—Biography.
Classification: LCC BX6193.W235 A3 2016 | DDC 289.9—dc23
LC record available at http://lccn.loc.gov/2015034830

To my Mother, Father,
Brothers, and Sisters,
for Eternal Love

We have been all along the Street called Straight,
where Saul of Tarsus was led after God struck him blind,
in Damascus. We even saw the place where they lowered
Paul through a high window in the wall, and he was let down
outside the city when he had to flee for his life.
Beyond doubt Paul went from there direct to Petra
where he spent the unaccounted for 3 years with Christ.
We thought of that, when we were in Petra—
and how undoubtedly that is the very place where
WE shall spend from 3 to 7 years during the Great Tribulation
and possibly also the terrible Day of the Lord, soon to come—
IF we are close to God instead of this pleasure-man world—
if we are praying always, and WATCHING, and accounted
worthy to escape the things that are coming on earth!

—Herbert W. Armstrong
Brethren & Co-Worker Letter

They were listening and paying attention
like he was God giving them a safe place to hide because
the world was coming to an end.

—Iceberg Slim
Pimp: The Story of My Life

PROLOGUE

A whistle from behind, the clomping of hooves. We moved close to the wall. Five mules lumbered past carrying tourists, led by boys much younger than my eleven- and thirteen-year-old sons. Our guide had warned us about the mules. They didn't always follow orders, he'd said, and there were no guardrails between the base of the mountain and Petra's monastery, eight-hundred-and-fifty steps above.

I'd planned to count the steps. I stopped at twelve. I was too busy worrying about my wife and our boys, none of whom was particularly athletic. I liked to think I was. But even so, at fifty, my knees weren't what they used to be. And the temperature was well over a hundred degrees, probably a hundred and thirty, assuming there is a wind-chill equivalent for blistering sun on stone.

The tourists who walked by us, going down, looked triumphant. Sometimes they encouraged us with nods and raised thumbs. One man told us the destination would be worth all the pain. We smiled and trudged on. Every once in a while we encountered local women beneath tents selling silk scarves, earrings and bracelets made of beads, handheld fans, water. We had water. Four bottles' worth. Thirty minutes into our trek, it felt warm enough to brew tea. We made the boys drink it anyway. Brenda and I drank it too. When we found unclaimed shade, we rested and I wondered if this was a good idea. Adrian, our oldest, looked as if he was about to faint; his cheeks had gone from cinnamon-brown to maroon. Dorian's mouth hung open like a fish long washed ashore.

We climbed. Occasionally, when the steps led us from the mountain's interior to unobstructed terrain, Brenda reminded the boys to take in the views. They gave cursory glances left and right before returning their attention to the ground, more interested in secure footing and avoiding dung than towering rock formations ringed in shades of red, the infinity of blue sky, and, two-thirds up, a ravine that wound into the brush where, we had been told, there was a tranquil holy spring as clear and delicate as glass.

Another whistle. This time the mules charged from above, barreling down on us at frightening speed, their passengers nowhere in sight, and for an instant I was certain they had toppled to their deaths, but then three little boys followed at full sprint, hooting and offering their services. As we stood pressed against the wall, Adrian asked how much longer. I told him I didn't know. The guide overheard me and said another thirty minutes. Brenda removed the water from my backpack, gave us a quick drink, poured some over our heads, and then we were off again. A few minutes later, when the boys complained of exhaustion, I decided to distract them with stories about my doomsday cult, even though they'd heard them before. But they would resonate more here.

PART 1

From the hall outside my parents' room I see my father lying on his bed. My mother is on the recliner by the window. They're both reading, their fingers gliding across large books that I know to be scripture. My mother already has on her dark glasses, supporting my suspicion that she sleeps in them. My father never wears dark glasses, supporting my suspicion that he can see. I take a deep breath and move forward, but I get a bad feeling about what I'm about to ask, and I decide to leave. As I back away the floorboard squeaks, and my fate is sealed.

"Who's that?" my father asks.

"Me."

"Jerry, what did I tell you about sneaking around the house?"

"I'm not sneaking around the house."

"Then what are you doing?"

"Walking around it normally."

He pushes himself up with his elbows. "Who's at the door this early in the morning?"

"On *Christmas*," my mother adds, compounding the infraction.

"Paul. He wants to know if Bubba and I can go to his house to play with his new toys."

They respond simultaneously, a split decision that means my father's yes trumps my mother's no. She asks him at what point during the night he lost his senses, and after he insists that a brief visit to Paul's can do no harm, she sighs and loses her senses too.

We wear pajamas beneath parkas, hoods over heads, our six boots crunching the frozen snow. A boy our age lives across the street, and I imagine him tearing through wrapping paper to get at his treasures. Houses in all directions are covered in lights; blues, reds, and greens spread over hedges, twisted around porch railings, spilled from gutters. Santas wave from some lawns and reindeer run through others. There are nativity scenes, of course, each one telling the story all wrong because Baby Jesus wasn't born in December. When my twin brother and I told this to our friends, they said it was a dumb reason not to celebrate Christmas. There had to be more to it, they figured, and after some discussion they decided Bubba and I had committed an act against our parents too shameful to reveal, and now we were being punished. We aren't being punished. We're being prepared for the Great Tribulation. In thirteen months, it will begin.

I once tried explaining that to Paul. "Well until it happens," he responded, "wouldn't you like some Hot Wheels?"

"Hot Wheels?"

He nodded.

"What kind of Hot Wheels?"

"Corvettes."

"Is that what you're getting for Christmas?"

"It's on my list," Paul said. And now, as we walk to his house, he reveals that Santa has come through.

When our doorbell rang a short while earlier, my heart leaped with a foolish thought that Santa had come through for me; foolish, because I've been told many times that he doesn't exist; foolish, because even if he does exist, our house is off limits; foolish, unless God ended the prohibition against Christmas and Santa was on my porch with an overstuffed bag, ready to make up for his six-year absence. I swung open the door, my disappointment at seeing Paul easing when he invited us to play with his toys. Bubba said we couldn't. I said maybe we could. He warned me that even asking our parents would be a sin against Jesus. I'm glad I didn't listen.

Paul's grandmother lives with him, having arrived one day from a place where women grow hair on their chins and hit children with wooden spoons. I hope we don't see her this morning, but she greets us at the door. As usual she wears a bandana over her hair, and her dark skin shines, like my father's dress shoes. "Take off your boots," she snaps, "before you track up the place with snow." We kneel to untie our laces. After a few seconds I glance up; she's frowning, even as she wishes Bubba and me merry Christmas. We wish her one back, as we've been instructed to do by our parents when given this greeting. But the phrase feels strange every time I use it, like some of the scripture I'm forced to memorize.

Paul has his boots off first. "Come on!" he yells, and he swoops down the basement stairs. Bubba is right behind him. I'm not right behind Bubba because my shoestring has a knot the size of a cherry. My foot is stuck. As I struggle to free it, Paul's grandmother asks about my parents.

"They're fine," I say.

"You being good to them?"

I glance up again. The light of an overhead fixture reflects off her wrinkled brow. She draws her nightgown around her, and I notice the handle of her spoon rising out of the left pocket.

"I'm very good to them," I say.

"You'd better be."

"I am."

"Come on!" Paul calls.

"They're blind, you know."

I say that I know.

She slowly shakes her head. "Haven't seen a day in their lives, God bless them."

This isn't true. My mother was born with a bad eye and accidently poked out the good one on a stick when she was nine, and my father lost his sight after falling down a flight of stairs when he was twelve. But I don't say this, because I've loosened my cherry knot and Bubba and Paul are revving their engines.

"Blind people need obedient sons."

That makes sense, I say.

"*Jerry!*" Paul yells. "What are you *doing* up there?"

His grandmother puts her hands on her hips. "You pick up after yourself?"

"Yes, ma'am."

"You come the first time they call?"

"Yes, ma'am."

Her eyes are nearly closed now, squinting against the glare of my white lies. "Well," she says at last, "go on then."

I run down the stairs, reaching the basement as Milo, Paul's eighty-pound German shepherd, is about to trot up. He has a turkey bone clamped between his teeth, though I don't give it much thought when, seeing the basement full of toys and overcome by what's in store, I wish him a merry Christmas and reach to pet his head.

The force of his impact knocks me off my feet. I lie on the floor stunned, not yet aware that I've been bitten until Paul's grandmother scrambles toward me, brings her hands to her face, and screams. I reach for my own face then, touching the blood and dangling flesh to the right of my lower lip, and scream too.

Then Bubba and Paul scream. Paul's parents scurry downstairs and ask what all the screaming is about, and after they scream, someone calls 911. By the time the paramedics arrive no one is screaming, but Paul's four-year-old sister is helping me cry. I've been carried to my living room, and everyone is here now—my parents and brothers and sisters, and Paul's parents and brothers and sisters and grandmother—everyone watching me being rocked on my mother's lap, hearing her soft assurances that I will be okay. And I believe her, not because God is merciful but because Paul, after the paramedics lift me from my mother's arms, presses a Corvette into my hand.

Nine stitches. The doctor who gives them to me says I'll have a permanent scar. Bubba gives me a scolding and says I have two more sins. My mother accepts responsibility for one of them, though, during bedtime prayers, asking God to forgive her for letting us go to Paul's. I lean toward her and whisper that she let me go to the emergency room too. But apparently that wasn't a sin this time. Even though we're forbidden from seeing doctors, she explains, sometimes God is too busy to heal us and expects us to take matters into our own hands. As an example, she uses my falling out of our second-story window.

I was two when it happened. We still lived on Chicago's West Side in the ABLA Homes, a housing project where people were often robbed or stabbed, apartments broken into, tires taken from cars. Sometimes, at night, we'd hear gunfire. One time when there wasn't any, Bubba and I were standing in our bedroom window with our faces pressed against the screen. Below us some kids were arguing over a toy, and then they started playing a game that called for running in circles and kicking an empty can. The third time their shadowy figures looped close to our building, I climbed onto the sill to get a better look, and now, in the blank space of my memory, I imagine hearing the screen *pop*, feeling it drop away, and suddenly Bubba is gone and I

see faces inches above mine asking if I am okay, telling each
other to stand back, to give me air. Someone warns that I
could have a fractured spine or a broken neck and shouldn't
be moved. This is disregarded. I am scooped from the dirt
and carried to our front door. Fists pound against it while a
chorus screams for my mother. . . .

My only injury was a cut on my left elbow, caused when
I brushed against the wall on the way to the ground. The
emergency-room doctors said I was very lucky. Later, at
home, my parents said God was very merciful. He protected
me from harm, they told me, and while I knew this was true, I
would've preferred him to simply snatch me from the window
when he saw me climb onto the sill. Then I wouldn't have
gone to the hospital, which, until now, I'd thought was a sin.

"Wait a minute," I say. "You mean that first hospital trip
didn't count?"

My mother says, "No, it didn't."

"Are you *sure* about that?" Bubba asks.

"I'm sure."

I think for a moment. "What about Linda's?"

"No," she says. "Hers didn't count either."

From what I recall being told of Linda's emergency trip
to the hospital, our two deacons had initially disagreed. They
came to our apartment to pray for her after she developed a
cough that wouldn't stop, even though my parents had prayed
for it to and had asked our congregation to pray with them.
The deacons' prayers didn't work either. By then Linda had
been coughing for nearly a month of the eleven she'd had,
but her first birthday didn't really come into question until
a few days before it arrived, when she started having trouble
breathing. The deacons returned, this time with oils, and after giving her a thorough anointing, they prayed over her crib

for three consecutive hours while she lay beneath them losing color. In the fourth hour of prayer, my father announced he was taking her to a doctor, and the deacons wiped away their tears and said a parent had to do what a parent had to do. But they advised him to keep what he was doing, as well as their role in it, a secret, which included driving my father and Linda at high speeds to the ER. One look at her limp body and the doctors had her on a gurney with a scalpel in her throat, slicing a path for air. She stayed in intensive care for the week it took God to finish doing whatever he was doing and to go to her bedside to place his mighty hand on her shoulder. After that, she opened her eyes, and it was okay to unplug the machines that had kept her alive.

That was in 1961, three years before Bubba and I were born. In 1968, we could have used God's healing powers again, only this time to save our baby brother. The morning our mother left to deliver him, her belly larger, it seemed, than Bubba and me combined, she let us press our ears against her navel to listen to his heart, and we placed our hands on her waist and felt his kick, and we put our lips on her ribs and told him we would see him soon. And as she was leaving, we cupped our hands to our mouths and shouted, "Winkle! Winkle! Winkle!" so he would know his nickname when we called it. But we didn't get to call it. Our mother came home from the hospital alone and said she'd lost him. For a long time after that she couldn't do much more than cry and moan.

Once, when I found her this way as she lay in her bed, I climbed in next to her. She put an arm around me, and I explained that Jesus loves babies so much that sometimes he brings them up to heaven. I gave her my biggest smile, even though she couldn't see it, and I waited for her to stop crying, but she cried harder. As she held me tightly against her, I added one more thing: just as soon as Jesus returns, all those dead babies will too.

Our mother has left our room. Bubba is asleep. I lie quietly in the darkness, my mind racing with the dawning awareness of some flexibility in how sins are determined. The way you think about a thing, the way you see it, could be what makes it right or wrong.

For a long time I remain awake thinking about the vegetables my mother serves with dinner, but there's no way for me to see how pretending I eat them is anything other than a lie, because I don't. I throw them behind the refrigerator, like Timmy taught me. We have to throw them there, because sometimes our mother, after inspecting our plates, her fingers nudging aside the chicken bones in search of hidden lima beans or pieces of broccoli, checks the garbage, where she once found his pile of beets, still warm.

The first few times I did it I felt guilty, but it helped if I made my bed without being asked, or dried the dishes, or used soap during my bath instead of just dunking the bar in the water. Twice, when I was very young, I drew her a picture. The first one was of the tall building around the corner from us where my cousins lived. That place wasn't safe either, especially when the elevators were broken and we had to share the stairwell with people who used it for things they weren't supposed to, none of them good. Sometimes, when I imagined Judgment Day, I saw sinners being led from elevators into that stairwell. I'd rather have eaten my vegetables than to go in there, but I'd learned that wasn't a deal God was willing to make.

The second picture was of a house, like the one my father was saving to buy us, putting a little away each month from his salary as a counselor at the Lighthouse for the Blind. When I held it in front of my mother and asked if she liked it, she set her needle and yarn next to her on the couch and said, "Jerry, do you remember what I told you about how Daddy and I see?"

I nodded.

"Do you?"

I nodded again.

"We see with our ears and our hands."

"And your feet," I reminded her.

"Yes, and our feet."

"And your canes."

"Our canes too. We see with many things, but not with our eyes. Our children are our eyes. That means you have to describe things to us, like I asked you to do with your picture last time. Can you describe this one for me too?"

I lowered it and turned it around. "It's a house," I said.

"What color is it?"

"Blue."

"Is it a big house?"

"Yes."

"Does it have a chimney?"

I forgot to draw a chimney. I shook my head, and for a while we were quiet.

"Did you shake your head?"

"Yes, ma'am."

"Honey," she said softly, "I've told you that when you want to tell Mommy and Daddy yes or no you have to *say* it instead of moving your head, because we can't *see* your head."

Unless she touched it, as she did every night, her fingers moving gently over my nose, cheeks, and lips before telling me I was handsome. I wouldn't have minded her doing that now, but I'd rather she liked my picture. Maybe she wouldn't like it, though, since it didn't have a chimney. I ran from the room, filling the apartment with noise because bells were tied to my shoes. Bubba's shoes had bells too. They let our parents know where we were, even when we kneeled and held them with our hands, or covered them with pillows, or rose to our tiptoes and walked extra slowly. We didn't have to wear the bells to church, because God always knew where we were and what we we're doing. But I hoped he wasn't paying attention while I was throwing away my vegetables.

When I returned, my mother asked if I had added a chimney. I nodded, and she said I'd better not be nodding, so I stopped. Then she reminded me that she ran into the stick that poked out her good eye because she'd disobeyed her mother. "You don't want God to make you blind, do you?"

I thought about being able to read books with my fingers, and of having my own white cane that pulled apart and folded into three pieces, and of gently touching my mother's nose, cheeks, and lips and telling her she was pretty. "Yes, ma'am," I said. "I want God to make me blind."

"No you *don't*," she responded, and her voice was sharp, like the one she used right before giving a spanking. "Don't *ever* say that. Don't *ever* want to be blind. And don't *ever* disobey your parents. Do you understand me?"

"Yes, ma'am."

She took a deep breath. We both did. Her voice was soft and nice again as she said my house was beautiful. We were both smiling now, and she wanted a hug. I gave her one before asking her to feel my face. "Now, my little handsome

boy," she said when she was done, "go show your picture to
Daddy." I ran to their bedroom, jingling my bells and calling
his name. After I described my house, he said we'd get one
exactly like it someday. But that spring it didn't seem we'd
have the chance, because Martin Luther King Jr. was killed,
and rioters set out to burn down the whole city. God had
his own fire planned, though, so he confined that one to
the West Side. For four whole nights, the gunfire we would
sometimes hear was replaced by sirens.

Two years later, in the summer of 1970, we bought the
house we're in when I make my second trip to the hospital.
It's something called a bungalow, and the neighborhood is
someplace called South Shore. A block away is a park with
swings and seesaws. A mile away is a beach. Grass and trees
line the streets, and none of the houses have bars on the
windows and doors. Before we moved my parents said there
wouldn't be any burglaries here. There wouldn't be any gunfire. We could play outside day or night without fear, unless what my aunt said about our new neighbors giving us
trouble was true. *Probably nothing but white folks over there*,
she warned us, and this was the case, except for Paul's family. They introduced themselves less than an hour after we
moved in and invited us to their backyard for a barbecue.
Bubba and I played with Paul that whole afternoon and later
made an assessment of his character. He's nice, we said. We
said he's fun. We said it's a shame he wasn't chosen. In two
years, we said, he'll be dead, just like our baby brother.

A deacon stands at the door like a sentinel, there to keep out strays. Bubba and I reach him first. We answer a couple of random questions about school before stepping past him and into the building. A narrow corridor flanked by wall-to-wall windows leads us to the outer lobby of the auditorium, where a smattering of adults quietly speak to each other. Nearby, children Bubba's and my age fidget in their suits and dresses, their hard, glistening shoes. Heads swivel in our direction. Two boys we know from Bible study say hello as we near them, and then they, like everyone else, look beyond us to watch our approaching parents. For some reason, blind people walking, or just breathing, is a thing of wonder.

When the rest of our family catches up, Bubba and I open the double doors on the right, releasing a drone of voices. Communing parishioners clog the aisles, and two-thirds of the five hundred seats are filled. I see eight empty ones together near the rear, where our father prefers to sit, and I lead us to them, forcing a smile when some adult thinks to rub my head or pat my shoulder. Behind me I hear people say hello to our parents extra loudly, which I know frustrates our father to no end. Once, when he and I were at Rexall Drugstore and the clerk shouted the cost of our Almond

Joys, Band-Aids, and Listerine, my father cracked, "Maybe you should repeat that, because I *still* can't see."

No sooner than we remove our coats and tuck them in our chairs, the lights blink. Conversations abruptly fall away, the aisles begin to clear. A minister makes his way to the stage. I brace myself, wishing I could plug my ears to block out his sermon. The ministers have always preached scary ones, but they've gotten worse as we approach the Great Tribulation. So last month Bubba and I began spending much of the three-hour services whispering to each other about our favorite superheroes and comic books. Later we got whippings that raised welts on our bottoms, but that was better than hearing the ministers' words, which have a way of coming back to you when it's time for bed.

This sermon is about the seventh of the seven plagues. Our parents won't let Bubba and me sit together anymore, so at the first mention of thunder and lightning I start counting the tiny ridges of my fingerprints. Next I count the ceiling panels. I count the folds in the curtain at the rear of the stage. I count the people in attendance and then I categorize them by age and gender and count them again. I count the short and skinny people; the fat people; the people who are friendly; the strange, bearded, and bald people; and the people who'll be crucified for getting divorced. I count the white people who'll be crucified for integrating our congregation rather than joining one of their own, but there are only three white people, so I count the sad comments I've heard about their spouses and children, who'll be crucified too for marrying interracially or being interracial. When I'm tired of counting, I try to nap like my father was until he snored and my mother nudged him as several parishioners looked our way, shocked that someone would steal a few winks while a great hail falls from heaven.

But I can't nap. The seat is too uncomfortable, though it's probably more comfortable than the wooden benches Paul says are in his church. Our seats are cushioned, and they have armrests with little tables that swing up from the sides, as you would expect to find in a high school auditorium, which is where we are. All the congregations around the country, and probably the world, rent similar kinds of places for worship. God wants us to keep our activities discreet, as if we aren't the Chosen Ones after all, but rather some random group of well-dressed people who like to read Bibles in schools.

When I was younger I thought God was just trying to conceal that he couldn't afford to build us churches. But I've since learned that he built us three colleges, two in the United States and another one in England. He bought us a jet too, so that his handpicked apostle and founder of our religion, Mr. Herbert W. Armstrong, could spread the true gospel around the world in grand style. Our God is not a poor God. Our God is a God of wealth. We are taught to see this as a point of pride.

I try to draw on this pride in times of despair, like when my parents can't afford to buy me a new toy, which is often. The church makes us keep three tithes: one to be saved for our Feast of Tabernacles celebration every fall, while the other two are sent directly to Mr. Armstrong's headquarters in Pasadena, California. Sometimes, in our local congregation, our ministers ask for a little more, and then the deacons fan out into the aisles carrying pails. When a pail reaches me, I hold up the quarter from my allowance and pause so everyone can see we aren't as poor as the families whose kids put in only pennies, nickels, and dimes. Once I found a dollar on my way to school and I put it in the pail. I thought God would be so pleased that he would keep the ministers' words out of my head that night, but I was wrong.

The sermon ends. We rise to sing the hymns. I like this part because my fourteen-year-old sister Mary has a lovely voice, and it distracts me from my thirteen-year-old brother Tommy's, which sounds like a frog. After the hymns, everyone sits again for the performance of the special song. I make my face blank as Mrs. Baker walks across the stage, the click of her heels keeping a steady rhythm until she reaches the piano. She doesn't bother telling us what she's about to play, because the song is for God, not us. But once it starts I know it's "Arise, Shine, for Thy Light Has Come," because my father listens to that some nights before he starts drinking his beer. When Mrs. Baker finishes, the room echoes with the song's beautiful sound, but we can't clap or smile, so I just pretend, along with everyone else, that she's done nothing more impressive than click her heels on the floor.

Now the head minister mounts the stage to deliver the main sermon. He sets his Bible on the podium and gazes slowly around the room, looking, I know, for me. After I've been found, he leans toward the microphone and asks who among us will have a rowboat and a paddle next year when the streets flow with fire. I reach for the scar Milo left me, nearly three weeks old. The stitches have been removed and the remaining indentation is soothing to touch. I glance at Bubba. He's concentrating on something on the back of his hand, his face an inch from his knuckles.

Nine hours later my bed is a lake of fire and I'm in it without a rowboat or a paddle. Even as my mother, Bubba, and I say our bedtime prayers I see myself struggling to tread waves of flames. Maybe Bubba sees himself struggling in that fire too, because after our mother kisses us and leaves the room, we lie quietly on our bunk beds for a long time— me on top, him on bottom—until he asks in a shaky voice if I want to sleep with him. Scrambling from the sheets, I nearly tear my legs from their sockets. Now our bodies are pressed so tightly together that there's space on the mattress for Tommy and Timmy if they decide to join us when they come upstairs. We left them in the living room watching *The Brady Bunch* with our sisters. Every once in a while some-one's laughter floats up to us, and it's a good thing to hear.

"I'm glad we're Chosen Ones," Bubba says.

I say, "Me too."

He pulls Mr. Bear closer, and I realize I left his twin, Mr. Teddy, on my pillow all alone in the darkness.

"I wish Paul was a Chosen One."

"So do I," I say.

Bubba mentions another boy from down the block. I mention a girl who lives across the street. Then we consider all our friends and classmates who we wish were chosen. We do this often, changing who's on the list based on our stand-ing with them at the time, but we always leave off Rodney Smith for calling us witches and Tony Hanks for being a bully. They're certain to find themselves in the lake of fire, and I know neither of them will have rowboats or paddles, not even after they've been resurrected during the millen-nium and given a second chance. I'll be a god by then— like all the Chosen Ones—and it'll be my responsibility to supervise the mortals' behavior, taking notes on whether they'll ultimately live or die. I'll try to be fair. And I won't abuse my superpowers, no matter how great they are. I hope to be able to fly and see through walls, but what I really want is a Captain America shield or a lightning bolt, like Captain Marvel's. I ask Bubba which he prefers.

"A lightning bolt," he says.

This is my first choice too.

"But a shield would be okay," he adds.

"Yeah, I'll take a shield, if that's all there is."

"I'm just glad I was chosen," he says again.

"Me too. It's going to be fun."

He nods.

"Unless," I note, "the devil breaks free of his chains."

"And releases some of those three-headed serpents?"

"Exactly."

"That would not be good."

"No, it wouldn't."

"Do you think God would let that happen?"

"I hope not."

"What if he's too busy to stop it?"

"Then we'll be in trouble."

"Big trouble."

"What if we get to have shields *and* lightning bolts?"

"Yeah, well, in that case we'll be fine."

"We'll be better than fine. We'll be *invincible*."

"*Invincible*," I repeat, "like Iron Man."

An understanding passes between us; this is a good place to stop. I fall asleep and dream of shields and lightning bolts and of paddling my rowboat through flames, sitting next to Paul. When I wake in the morning I feel so good about the Great Tribulation I almost wish it had happened already. I ease myself from the sheets, careful not to disturb Bubba. Tommy and Timmy's bunk bed is already empty, I notice, as I climb up the ladder. When I mount the fourth rung, I

can see Mr. Teddy on his back, looking afraid, his tiny paws
outstretched, reaching for my hands.

In the kitchen I pour a bowl of Fruit Loops, skipping the
milk, and carry it to the living room. Linda's on the floor
mediating a conflict between two dolls. Mary reclines on
the couch lazily flipping the pages of a magazine. Before
sitting next to her I turn on the television and Bullwinkle's
deep voice fills the room with jokes he's told before. When
his show is over, *Dudley Do-Right* comes on. It's a rerun too,
and followed by another episode of *Rocky and Bullwinkle*, the
same one I have just seen. I know from surveying *TV Guide*
that a wide variety of cartoons air on Saturday mornings,
but we can't watch television or do much of anything from
sunset Friday to sunset Saturday because this is our Sabbath,
like it is for Jehovah's Witnesses. I don't know who Jehovah
is, but I know that the boys who make fun of me for witnessing him aren't on my list to be saved.

Friday evenings we usually read or play Scrabble, and
Saturday, after church and until dusk, we do the same.
By the time Sunday morning finally rolls around, Dudley
Do-Right and Bullwinkle reruns are pretty good options.
Sometimes I think it's fun to speak the characters' lines with
them, or move my lips while they say the words. I'm doing
this with Rocky when Bubba comes into the room with a
bowl of Crunch Berries and sits next to me. If we were a
little older, we wouldn't have to amuse ourselves this way,
because we could play on the church's peewee basketball
team, and practice is Sunday mornings. Timmy and Tommy
are twelve and thirteen and on the team for older kids. They
practice Sunday afternoons. They usually watch cartoons

with Bubba and me, but earlier, when I passed the dining room, I saw them playing chess. I go to watch them.

Tommy's hunched over the board, a hand above his eyes in salute. Timmy's smiling, so I figure he's about to win, especially when he pulls out the chair next him and pats the cushion for me to come get a better view. As I take it, Tommy nudges one of his pieces forward. Timmy replaces it with one of his. "And that," he says, "is checkmate."

Tommy studies the board for a moment. "How did I miss that?" he asks.

"Good question," Timmy says. He offers a rematch. Tommy declines. Before leaving, he tells me he won two of their four matches. "Barely," Timmy adds. He slides the board between us and sets up the pieces. I'm still learning the rules, whereas he's an expert, thanks to grandmaster Bobby Fischer. When Fischer converted to our faith several years ago, Timmy became obsessed with the game. He's obsessed with Fischer too, and quotes him nearly as much as he quotes the Bible. He's quoting Fischer now: "'A strong memory, concentration, imagination, and a strong will are required to become a great chess player.'"

I pick up one of the white pieces. "What is this one called again?"

"A pawn." And then more Fischer: "'I like the moment I break a man's ego.'"

I pick up another piece, the one with the circular top that resembles a castle. "How does this one move?"

"Front to back, side to side." And then Fischer: "'Chess is war over the board. The object is to crush the opponent's mind.'"

"This one?"

"Diagonally." And then: "'Chess is life.'"

I shake my head. "Chess is *confusing*," I say. "Life is simple."

And then it's June, and suddenly life is confusing too. Bubba and I have just come home from school to find a little boy on our mother's lap, smiling and clutching one of his red socks in his chubby hand. We stand frozen in the doorway, our heads snapping back when she calls him *Winkle*. We rush to them on the couch and say we're home. Our mother tells us to greet our baby brother, and we do, but a part of me is afraid to touch him because I think he might be the devil, here to lure me into sinning again. So before I hug him, I put my hand on the back of his head, checking for the nub of horns.

A man is here too. He sits across from our parents on the loveseat, a mysterious figure I vaguely registered a moment ago, but now I study his thin frame, short and well-groomed Afro, the dark glasses that indicate he's blind, the cigarette that indicates he's a heathen. "Say hello to Bill," our mother says. Bill scoots to the edge of his seat and extends his hand. After Bubba and I shake it, our mother tells us to take Winkle to the basement to play.

Once we're downstairs, I inspect him more thoroughly until I'm mostly satisfied he isn't the devil. I ask him how old he is. He responds with fingers. Three. He's my three-year-old baby brother. My three-year-old baby brother who's been returned to us by a blind heathen named Bill. A thought pops into my head: *Bill is Jesus*. Jesus disguised as a blind, black heathen—this I can almost understand. But I can't understand the smoking, unless the smoke isn't really smoke, only an illusion to further conceal the Lord's identity. This is a lot for me to take in, so I give up trying and instead focus on helping Winkle stack the cans of beans and corn we're storing for the Great Tribulation.

One by one my siblings race to the basement to meet our baby brother. Linda and Mary go crazy over him, repeatedly kissing his fat cheeks and saying he looks like me, which he does, except he doesn't have a scar. Tommy and Timmy wrestle with him. Bubba and I tickle his feet and pull his toes. We're having a good time. Then our mother tells us Winkle has to leave, and I can't understand this either.

Now we're all in the living room taking turns hugging Winkle good-bye while Jesus waits at the door puffing his fake cigarette. Outside, a taxi driver leans against his car. (Later, I'll wonder if *he* was Jesus.) Mary and Linda are quietly sobbing. Our mother is too, though as soon as Jesus takes Winkle's hand and leads him away, she composes herself enough to tell Bubba and me to come with her to her bedroom.

She closes the door behind us. We sit next to her on the bed as she explains that Winkle didn't stay in heaven because too many babies were already there. So he was sent to an orphanage, where Bill adopted him. Bill is his parent now.

I ask for a clarification. "Is Bill Jesus?"

"No," our mother responds.

"He's not?"

"No, Jerry."

"And Winkle isn't Satan?"

"Of course not. He's your baby brother."

Her voice trembles. I understand she won't be able to continue much longer, so I rush to what really matters. "Is Winkle coming back?"

There's a pause. "Yes," she says.

"When?" Bubba asks.

Another pause. "When he can."

"Tomorrow?" Bubba presses.

"No, not tomorrow."

"*When?*" I ask.

But she's crying hard now and can't speak, so I have to wait until tonight to get my answer, when Winkle appears on the field during my baseball dream. I remove my catcher's mitt to take his hand, and then we are in my basement again stacking the cans of beans and corn. I tell him I'm glad he has returned from the dead. He says he's glad he has returned too. I tell him I'm especially glad he's not Satan, though I would feel more confident of this, I explain, if his eyes weren't circles of light, and if he hadn't grown horns. "Are you *positive* you're not Satan?" I ask. He says yes, he's positive he's not Satan. He's just my baby brother.

Our father forbids us from mentioning Winkle's name and our mother tells us to put him out of our minds, which aren't easy to do until a month later, when we get a new baby brother and a puppy. We name the puppy Pepper. We name the baby Michael. Michael is with us for two weeks. We were warned that someone could come for him at any time because he's a foster child, with us only on loan, but it's still terrible to see him go. Then we get another baby and name this one Charles. Charles is taken away four days later. After this, I keep expecting someone to come for Bubba or me, or for one of our brothers or sisters, but another month passes and we're all still here. Now we have to make it only six more months, to the Great Tribulation, when the droughts, famine, and wars begin and the unconverted writhe in the streets, their bodies covered with the boils illustrated in one of Mr. Armstrong's booklets, which are even scarier to look at, I think, than to hear our ministers' sermons.

In November, with two months to go, I decide to give a sermon of my own. The service is held in my basement. The congregation is Paul. I hope that if I can convert him to the true word of God, then he can convert his parents, and they can all be spared the torture and suffering headed their way. I clear my throat and glance at my construction paper. I have jotted down some notes. "How would *you*," I shout, "like to be covered in boils?"

"I wouldn't like that at all," he says.

I peer over my construction paper. "You're not supposed to answer me."

"You asked me a question."

"That was just my title."

"Well, I already know how I feel about being covered in boils, so you don't need to preach anymore."

"But do you know how to *avoid* being covered in boils?"

"I don't have any yet, so I guess I do."

"You'll be getting some soon if you don't be quiet and listen."

"What are boils, anyway?"

"Sores."

"I know that, but what kind of sores? Like blisters?"

"I think so. Only worse."

"How?"

"They hurt really bad."

"Blisters hurt really bad too. My grandmother had one on her left big toe and she could barely get off the couch without cussing."

"The boils I'm talking about are worse than that. These can kill you."

"Blisters can too if you don't treat them with iodine. Bet that'd work on them boils."

I excuse myself and go upstairs. A moment later I return with Mr. Armstrong's booklet *1975 in Prophecy* and show Paul the illustration that served as the inspiration for my sermon. Beneath it a caption reads, "Unrepentant human beings will be stricken with excruciatingly painful boils—no position of the body may give relief from their agonies—as

God destroys the evil works of sinning mankind to bring the nations to repentance."

"I guess there's no iodine in hell," Paul says.

"This is earth. Hell doesn't exist yet."

"Course it does."

"No it doesn't."

"It *does*. My grandmother talks about it all the time, and when people upset her, she recommends them to it."

"That doesn't mean it's real."

"Tell that to my grandfather. He's there now. My grandmother says it's the reward he earned for telling lies and drinking White Lightning."

"Your grandmother's wrong," I say. "I bet she doesn't know the truth about heaven either."

"She knows she's going to it, and me too one day, if I can ever remember to come the first time she calls."

"Does she know heaven is moving down here?"

"To *Chicago*?"

I see a chance to get my sermon back on track. All I have to do is switch the topic from boils to the Kingdom of Heaven. I should've gone with that in the first place because it is fresh in my memory. My parents record Mr. Armstrong's sermons from his radio program, and earlier today I heard parts of one they listened to about the Kingdom of Heaven being right here on earth soon. Jesus will rule it and we'll all be happy. No one is happy now. Not like they were when Mr. Armstrong was a boy on an Iowa farm. Back then the farmers would plow their land with mules, because they didn't have tractors, and even though the work was hard, the farmers would sing all day long. That kind of happiness is behind us, gone forever, and now the world is full of misery. Until our spiritual problems are solved we will continue to be miserable, and they won't be solved up in heaven, because heaven will be down here. This is what I tell Paul. "What do you think?" I ask. "Makes sense, doesn't it?"

"Well, I have to admit," he says, "I've never seen no farmers singing behind mules."

"Exactly."

"And I do feel kind of sad sometimes, like when I have to go to school. But I've never been *miserable*."

I narrow my eyes. "Never?"

"Never."

I guess he's forgotten about last summer. After striking out four times in a single baseball game, he cried for the entire block-long walk home. And I cried too. I desperately want to play Little League baseball, but the games are on Saturdays and playing sports during the Sabbath isn't allowed. We can't even watch the games. The only reason I saw Paul's strikeouts was because I volunteered to take Pepper for a walk, which just happened to lead me to the park in time for the season opener. All the players wore their pristine uniforms and baseball caps. Some of them had new gloves. And for the first time the bats were aluminum; the *ping* they made when striking the ball was like music, a special music for boys instead of God. I would've given anything to produce that sound. After the game ended and Paul collapsed into his mother's arms, I knew he would've given anything too. But I don't remind him of this now. It would upset him. Even though I've been a minister for only ten minutes, I know an upset congregation is harder to save than one with amnesia. So I drop the subject of misery and return to the real one at hand: "Do you accept the true word of God," I ask, "now that you've heard it?"

"I don't know," he says. "I need to think about it for a while."

I remind him of the boils.

"How much time do I have to decide?"

"Until January seventh."

"That's when Jesus is returning?"

"No. Jesus is returning in 1975. January seventh in 1972 is when the earthquakes, drought, famines, boils, and stuff will start."

"Why are they starting before Jesus is here to watch?"

I don't know. There's something about nineteen-year cycles and the Holy Roman Empire. And the pope. But I'm not sure how it all fits together. So I say, "It's in the Bible."

"Locusts are in the Bible. Will there be some locusts?"

"*Of course* there'll be locusts!"

His eyes widen, as if the locusts are swarming out of the storage room behind me. I glance over my shoulder before continuing. "But we don't have to worry about any of that, because right before the Tribulation starts we'll leave."

He looks around my basement. "With all this corn and beans?"

"That's for here, in case our leaving is delayed for some reason. There won't be any food in the stores, so this is what we'll live on."

"What's going to happen to the food in the stores?"

"Looters will take it."

"So you're going to be hiding in the basement eating beans and corn until Jesus returns?"

"No, just until we leave. We might leave on time so we won't need to take anything. I guess there'll be food there."

"Where?"

"In the Place of Safety."

"Where's that?"

I can't remember what it's called, only that it's in a desert. I tell him the Sahara.

"And you have to stay there forever?"

"Just for three and a half years."

"Three and *a half* years? Why three and a half years?"

"It's in the Bible."

He nods.

"And then," I continue, "Jesus will rise again and turn us into gods so we can fly around chasing down sinners." I mention the strong likelihood of getting lightning bolts or shields.

"Boy," he says, "my parents sure picked the wrong religion."

"We didn't pick it. It picked us. And it's picking you right now." I remember something Mr. Armstrong often says and repeat it: "God is speaking to *you* through *me*."

"And he's telling me to live in the Sahara Desert eating beans and catching sinners?"

"The beans are for *here*."

"The *corn* is for the desert?"

"No, that's for here too."

He shakes his head. "This is really confusing."

It is really confusing. I'm confused all the time. "Basically," I say in conclusion, "our church is like chess."

"I don't know how to play chess. Will I have to learn?"

"You can if you want. There's no rule or anything that says you have to. The only rule is that you accept the true word of God that I'm giving you."

He rises from his chair and moves toward the stairs. "I don't know. It's a lot to think about. And I have to ask my dad."

"Tell him about the boils."

"I will."

Before he leaves, he makes me promise that he'll get either a lightning bolt or a shield. I tell him I might be able to arrange for him to get both. His eyes widen again, and I know my sermon was successful. So when he comes back a few minutes later, I'm surprised to hear him say his parents didn't accept God's call, and so he's stuck being a Baptist. Now he's definitely miserable, but I don't point it out this time either. I put my hand on his shoulder and tell him when I figure the boils have started covering his body, probably sometime in February, I'll pray for God to show him mercy. And once my family is gone, I add, he can help himself to our leftover beans and corn.

When I tell my parents about my sermon to Paul, they get upset, even more so when I say that all I did was open my mouth and the words of God emerged. My father says it was as likely the devil who moved my lips, because we're not supposed to spread the gospel. If people show an interest in our faith, we're instructed to have them listen to *The World Tomorrow* radio and television broadcasts.

My parents' instructions came from Randall McKenzie, who was black and blind too. He and my father had been friends at the Sight Saving School in Jacksonville, Illinois, where my father was sent when he was sixteen. They remained friends after moving back to Chicago to work at the Lighthouse for the Blind. My father met my mother there in 1954. A year later they were married in her longtime storefront Sanctified Church, where every Sunday they returned to worship a false god and speak in tongues.

One day, when my father was moved to speak in tongues from the pulpit in addition to the pew, he became the congregation's second ordained minister. His sermons were powerful, my mother has said, often sending the congregation into fits and wails of prayer, something the other minster wasn't skilled enough to do, though he came close one Sunday when two pregnant teenagers rose and identified him as their expected babies' father. He denied it, but the accusations were enough to have my parents consider other possibilities of worship, even that peculiar one favored by Randall.

So they followed his advice and listened to the church's broadcasts, but they didn't know what to make of them. The host was an elderly white man. He did not sing. He did not speak in tongues. There was no Holy Ghost to catch or healing hands to lay. Instead, he offered logic, reason, and a charismatic personality, backed by the mind of a meticulous scholar. There was fear in the threat of death for failing to heed God's call. There was hope in the promise of restored sight at the moment of Christ's return.

They listened to more sermons. They bought reel-to-reel versions of Mr. Armstrong's Bible studies and fell asleep to descriptions of how and when the final hours would unfold. They prayed, first with each other, then with Randall, and then with Randall's deacon, who came to their apartment to confirm they had indeed been chosen, and to warn them of the consequences they could expect upon refusal to agree. They did not refuse, especially after the deacon explained that as many as 95 percent of converts were white; so when black folk were called, it was because God had concluded they were *extra* worthy. My parents joined Randall's congregation in the summer of 1960.

And through it all, Randall hadn't preached to them once, because preaching to friends is a sin, and having friends at all, unless they're already converted, is just shy of being another one. We're strongly advised not to socialize with people not of our faith, but socializing with people *of* our faith isn't always easy. Our congregation draws from many black communities, and none of its brethren live particularly close to us. I'm pretty certain Paul is the first heathen any kid in my family has been allowed to have as a close friend. I don't know why my parents made this exception, but I'm glad they did. So even if it is a sin to try to save him, it is a worse sin, it seems to me, not to try.

B anned from preaching, I consider writing Paul a letter like the ones Mr. Armstrong writes church members once a month. He often composes them while flying on his jet, each letter greeting us as "Co-Workers," as if we're in the business of making shoes instead of saving souls. The letters include analyses of the Bible and some of its hidden meanings, but they're mainly important because they keep us current on where we are regarding the Great Tribulation and exactly what he's doing to keep it on schedule. Mr. Armstrong's job is to pave the way for Jesus's return by spreading God's message all over the world. Our job is to pay for the spreading.

A few years ago my parents bought a globe so we could track Mr. Armstrong's travels, and in this way I learned the location of places like Singapore, Indonesia, Australia, and China. Then they bought the *Encyclopedia Britannica* and I read a little about the people in these countries and their cultures. Sometimes this information comes in handy, like when my teacher mentioned New Zealand and asked if anyone had heard of it, or when we had a spelling test that included the words Turkey and Manila. Other times the information makes me sad. I think it would be interesting to visit some of these places as an adult, but ever since I was a baby I've known I'll never get to be an adult. By the time the Tribulation is over and Christ returns, I'll only be eleven.

But the first week of January 1972 comes and goes and the Tribulation hasn't even started. When we receive the newsletter later in the month there's no mention of it at all. Then it's February, and our minister reads a statement from Mr. Armstrong insisting he never set dates, as he insisted two years ago. At that point, talk of his prophesied 1972 end-times had reached a fever pitch, including in our household, so we were surprised when we received the September newsletter that read:

Many Brethren have somehow gained the FALSE idea that we have said our Work will definitely be finished then, and we will at that time be taken to the place of safety and protection. WE HAVE NEVER SET THAT OR ANY OTHER DATE, except as a POSSIBLE one. There is NO PROPHECY pointing definitely to that date. There have been a number of INDICATIONS of it as a POSSIBLE date, and the first one we consider at all likely. Right now it looks to me as about a 50–50 chance, and at least 50–50 our Work may go on another 5 or 10 years.

Some Brethren have gained the idea Mr. Meredith said DEFINITELY it would go on 5 or 10 more years. Mr. Meredith told me he merely tried to correct the idea of a January 1972 date as a CERTAINTY. IT IS NOT A CERTAINTY! No date is, but the January 1972 date is, in my judgment, STILL A POSSIBILITY.

Yesterday, for the second time in two or three days, Jordanian guerrillas made another attempt to assassinate

King Hussein. This morning's news says Iraq is threatening to attack Jordan. Such an event might trigger a chain reaction that would cause events to happen SO FAST, that what we have thought possible for January, 1972 can easily yet happen. In fact, events could go on ANOTHER YEAR from now, with nothing startling happening, then suddenly lightning moves in Europe and the Middle East could bring everything to a climax by January 1–7, 1972.

IT STILL MAY HAPPEN THEN. Also it may not happen for 5 to 10 years. ABOVE ALL, REMEMBER WE CANNOT SET ANY DATES!

I didn't know who Mr. Meredith was, but I knew I'd rather there be five or ten years left instead of two. But for my parents, the *possibility* of two was good reason to expect it; so his letter was disregarded, as is the statement he had our minister read today. As soon as we get home from church, my parents note that Mr. Armstrong is eighty years old and make jokes about the *possibility* of his senility, and then they assure us that the Tribulation is still near. But there's nothing for them to joke about when the March newsletter doesn't mention it either. Their mood improves in April, though, when we get a strong indication that terrible events are finally upon us. Satan, Mr. Armstrong writes, has captured his son.

His son's name is Garner Ted Armstrong. He's the host of *The World Tomorrow* television broadcast and runs Ambassador College in Pasadena, as well as the church's magazine, *The Plain Truth*. My father says if you destroy Garner Ted, you'll destroy God's work; so in capturing

Garner Ted, the devil knew exactly what he was doing. We, on the other hand, do not know exactly what Garner Ted did to be captured. Mr. Armstrong's letter is vague about the sins his son committed, mentioning only that they're serious enough for him to take a leave of absence to repent and pray. They're also serious enough for our congregation to lose some of its members. Not as many leave this time, though, as they did in January, when the Tribulation didn't start.

Even Paul wondered about the boils. He, Bubba, and I were walking home from school, a blustery February wind at our backs, when Paul suddenly stopped and asked, "So what do I do with my iodine?" He stole it from his grandmother, he said, back in December, and now he felt stupid for doing so. I tried to console him by saying the boils were still coming, but he didn't need consoling. He admitted that he was grateful for the delay and hoped the entire Tribulation would be called off, like a baseball game due to rain. I guess I hoped that as well, since what I felt was closer to Paul's gratitude than the disappointment that caused some Co-Workers to leave the church. And if my parents said we were leaving the church too, I wouldn't have objected.

But I doubt my parents will ever leave. I am certain of it when Mr. Armstrong sends two more newsletters, one explaining that Garner Ted has been freed, the other explaining why the Tribulation has been delayed. Before it can start, Mr. Armstrong writes, he has to spread the gospel more thoroughly around the world, as prophesied in Malachi 3:1, the scripture he quotes and orders us to read. "Behold," it says, "I will send my messenger, and he shall prepare the way before me: and the Lord, whom ye seek, shall suddenly come to his temple." Mr. Armstrong does not know how much additional time he has been given, but one thing is clear: there are signs, more and more every day, that God won't contain his wrath for long.

ometimes, when I put my ear to the gap beneath my parents' bedroom door, I can hear them talking. If I am lucky, they are talking about me, but usually the subject is money, as it was a second ago before I sneezed. Now the room has gone silent, but before I can crawl away the door is snatched open. My father stands before me in boxers and a T-shirt, his stomach as big as my mother's on the day of Winkle's birth and death. "Who's here?" he asks. I don't answer. He moves forward, pausing only inches from my hands, as if it's Passover and I've come in humility to wash his feet. It's only a regular Friday morning, though, and I've come in sin.

"Who's out here?"

I still don't respond. He takes another step. One more and I'll be discovered. I hold my breath and watch his left foot slowly rise and then settle on my fingers, pressing them into the carpet.

"Good morning, Daddy," I say.

From behind him my mother asks, "Jerry?"

"Who else?" my father answers.

I pull my fingers free and rise. For a brief moment my father and I stand chin to beer belly before he moves past me and into the bathroom, leaving my mother to carry out the interrogation. "Jerry, what did we tell you about your sneaking?"

"I wasn't sneaking?"

"What did we tell you about your lying?"

"*I'm not lying*," I say, and then I lie about hearing a squeak and lowering myself to search for a mouse, the very one, most likely, that gnawed a hole in the toe of my canvas sneakers.

The toilet flushes. My father comes out of the bathroom and takes sides with God and my mother. "God sees you disobeying us," he says. "And he sees you lying."

Now he sees me crying, I think, as I imagine the punishment I have in store.

"Go wake your brothers and sisters," my father tells me. "I'll deal with you after school."

At school I'm a prayer zombie, drifting through the day's lessons while begging God to have my father change his mind. This worked once before. I was caught eating a slice of cheese without permission, which, in my parents' view, is stealing, and my father sent me to my room saying he'd call me when he was ready. The next morning I woke still fully clothed, my face pressed against the open pages of my Bible, smearing the book of Matthew. I don't know why he spared me, especially since theft is such a serious offense. Our faith commands that children receive corporal punishment for much less.

Parents take this command seriously. Sometimes children come to church with bruises, or they limp down the aisle, wincing as they lower into their seats. After the service they tell stories about having tripped down the stairs or been dinged with the cork of a champagne bottle, or how they walked into the path of a moving vehicle. We don't press them for details, because we know these are lies, since we tell them ourselves. And as men mill about in the lobby, they speak openly of the rod that wasn't spared. I heard one father say he favors his palm, because he likes the sound of skin on skin; another said he uses a paddle with holes cut into the wood to reduce wind resistance. Then there was the man who boasted that he uses stones, taken from the bed of his wife's prized flower garden, but after a beat he doubled over in laughter, so it was hard to know if what he said was true.

Every once in a while we hear rumors of someone going too far, resulting in a child's serious injury. When I missed a week of services after Milo bit me, and reappeared with a freshly stitched wound on my face, that was the rumor about me. One boy couldn't contain himself and confronted me directly. "I heard your dad *really* let you have it," he said, and because it wasn't a question I didn't give an answer. Besides, a part of me liked the idea of my father's blindness not being held against him, that his inability to see has not affected his manhood. And for our church, disciplining children—and wives too, for that matter—is as much about manhood as it is about discipline; hardly a sermon passes without a minister quoting 1 Timothy 3:5: "For if someone does not know how to manage his household, how will he care for God's church?" But even as an eight-year-old, I know managing one's household can be done with fear as well as force; maybe that was my father's lesson when he'd spared me. I hope he'll offer that lesson again.

After school I do my homework as usual, play with Bubba in the backyard as usual, read for a while as usual, and volunteer to help my mother prepare dinner and to shine my father's shoes, which aren't usual. When neither parent mentions my transgression, I wonder if I'm in the clear.

When my father laughs at my knock-knock joke during dessert, it seems to be a good sign. But the most encouraging signs are that I make it through my bath and bedtime prayers. In the five minutes between my mother kissing me goodnight and my father calling me, I manage, for the first time all day, to relax.

He calls me again. I ease from my sheets and climb over the bunk bed's rail. When I reach the ladder's bottom rung and register the concern in Bubba's eyes, any thoughts of being spared seep away. On the stairs I move like a sloth; so when I finally reach the bottom step, I've managed to summon a small amount of hope for a stern talk, but this vanishes when I pass the living room and none of my siblings look my way. Right before I enter my parents' bedroom, my mother walks out, the tips of her fingers grazing the wall as she moves toward the kitchen. I clear my throat by way of greeting, a dryness in my mouth making it impossible to speak.

My father closes the door behind me. He sits in the recliner and tells me to strip below the waist, lie facedown on the bed, and be quiet. I obey the first two orders, but I can't manage the third, not as Bubba once did, even after his punishment started. Before we were called to our father to answer for some offense, Bubba swore he wouldn't cry. At first I stood by the side of the bed in admiration of his resolve, and then I watched in horror when it so angered our father that his belt began to whiz as it cut through the air. Bubba cried eventually, ear-piercing wails that convinced me not to duplicate his approach, so I released ear-piercing wails before I was hit. That angered our father even more. Now I'm crying measuredly, hoping to strike the right balance between genuine regret and theater.

Across my father's lap is a volume of scripture. I close my eyes as he starts to read. *"Whoever spares the rod hates his son, but he who loves him is diligent to discipline him."* Pages turn. *"Do not withhold discipline from a child; if you strike him with a rod he will not die."* Pages turn. *"Folly is bound in the heart of a child, but the rod of discipline drives it far from him."* The thump of the closed volume. The release of the recliner's springs. The creak of the floor. The jangle of the belt buckle. Leather, slithering through the loops of pants. Screams. Pleas. Apologies, first mine, then his.

Satan, once I'm back in bed, filling my thoughts with hate. I hold on to them for five days before forgiving my father and accepting responsibility for my actions. I shouldn't have been sneaking around the house. The punishment was just. My heart was bound with folly and I deserved to have it driven out. God hears my repentance. I know this because he rewards me for it in the spring.

S ears and Roebuck split finger, lacing between the fingers and a tunnel pocket; a present for his eleventh birthday. He's told us how he used to sleep with it beneath his pillow every night while dreaming of playing shortstop like his hero Luke Appling. The dreams didn't stop the following year when my father lost his sight, and his love of baseball grew stronger. Listening to the sport, to all sports, in time, took his mind off his handicap. It still does. If a game is being played, he is likely to have it on the radio, unless it's the Sabbath, and even then there are times when Harry Carey or Bill Mercer can be heard whispering beneath my parents' door. Sometimes, when my father calls from his room for someone to bring him another beer, we find him sitting on the side of his bed, an empty mug in one hand, his glove on the other.

He won't let us use it. He uses it, though, whenever he plays catch with us in the backyard. He'll stand with his gloved hand extended in front of him, the arm bent at the elbow like a hobo begging for coins, and we try to toss the ball into the pocket, stepping farther away with each success, a little closer with each fail. When he tosses it back we help him locate us by saying, "Right here" or "This far." One day while we were playing, Paul came upon us and froze with his mouth open because the only thing he knew about blindness was what I told him the day we met.

"How did your father get blind?"

"He fell and hit his head when he was twelve."

"Did your mother fall too?"

"No. She was born without one good eye and had an accident with the other."

"How old was she when she had the accident?"

"Nine."

"Does your father wear dark glasses?"

"No."

"Why not?"

"He doesn't like them."

"Does your mother have eyes?"

"No, not really."

"What does she have?"

"Gray stuff."

"What do you mean?"

"What I said. Gray stuff."

"Shaped like eyes?"

"No."

"What shape is the gray stuff?"

"It doesn't really have a shape."

"It must have a shape."

"It doesn't."

"That sounds spooky."

"It's not."

"Not even a little?"

"A little. But we're used to it."

"Is that why she wears dark glasses, so she doesn't spook people?"

"I guess so."

"She wears them in the house too?"

"Usually."

"Has she seen you before?"

"No."

"Have you told her what you look like?"

"She knows."

"How does she know?"

"She feels my face. She knows I am handsome."

That satisfied him. But after he saw our father playing catch he wanted to know more. So Bubba and I explained that our parents read with their fingers, and we let him examine their stylus and slate and their Brailler typewriter. We showed him their labeller and pointed to our stove and washing machine where the dials were marked. We let him taste the fried chicken our mother knew was done by listening to the oil, and we explained how she matched her clothes by memorizing their colors based on the feel of fabric, or by marking them with safety pins. We told him our father finds his way to and from the bus stop by noting changes in the sidewalk—the rises and the dips, the potholes, the buckles made by the roots of large trees. We told him about the bells we once wore on our shoes and even the funny story we heard of how Mary, when she was a baby, thought the only way to search for something on the floor was by crawling on it and patting her hands like she'd seen our parents do. We unlocked mystery after mystery of blindness for Paul so that by the time God rewards me for my repentance with my first White Sox game, Paul thinks nothing of a blind man being at Comiskey Park.

Other people do. As Bubba and I walk with our father from the train station in the crowd of fans, I can feel the staring. The staring upsets me. It always does. That's why I try never to make eye contact with anyone when I'm in public with my parents. But now, when we reach the gate, I can't help but look at the boy to my right who says, "There's a blind man." He's three or four years old, and he's pointing. The man he's with pushes down his arm. The boy looks from my father to me, his face full of concern, as if my own blindness is about to take hold. Sometimes I wish it were. Then I wouldn't have to see people react to my parents like they're the man with two faces and the four-legged woman, circus freaks I once glimpsed in a book of human oddities. And I wouldn't have to experience the embarrassment that being with my parents sometimes makes me feel. Or the shame that follows.

We're inside the park. Our father tells us to find an usher, so now I have to pay attention to the people around me, and what I see is different from what I am used to. There are smiles, cocked heads, raised eyebrows. Looks of amusement rather than pity, as if we've made a silly mistake by coming here. At first we even get it from the usher, a chubby, bearded man whose eyes bug out as we approach. But as they slowly lower into slits, I wonder if it's dawning on him that we're here to cause trouble, and I wish my father could accommodate him, that he had the power to toss his cane to the ground, like Aaron tossed Moses's staff, and transform it into a serpent. Or maybe, since our seats are in the upper balcony, the usher thinks he'll be held responsible if my father tumbles over the rail. And maybe the fans we pass think that before falling my father will pull them with him, so they give us wide berth, even wider, it seems, than what we're given when we board city buses or trains or walk along busy streets.

The seats are good. We're right on the first base line, four rows in, and in the warmth of the April sun. After the national anthem our father takes his transistor radio and earplugs from his jacket pocket to listen to the play by play. Soon he's cheering and complaining along with the crowd. I try to forget about the stares and concentrate on enjoying myself like he is, even though I know he must have heard the boy. He's used to it, I guess. I guess it doesn't bother him. I'm not bothered by it either, I tell myself, which is true by the time Bubba and I eat a bag of roasted peanuts and two boxes of Cracker Jack. Now we're sitting on the edge of our seats, hoping that every hit ball comes our way. We have on our gloves. Our father has on his. No one is paying us any attention. They're focused on the game, calling for Goose Gossage to throw strikes. "Right down the middle, Goose!" our father yells, followed by Bubba's echo, then mine.

T he deacons rotate among the parishioners' houses for Sabbath dinner. Tonight is our turn to host. From the serving of the salad to the second slice of peach cobbler, the adults do all the talking, every word related to the Bible. Afterward, we go to the living room for the night's entertainment, which is related to the Bible too, but now the children hold the floor.

We stand along the wall arranged from oldest to youngest. Our mother tells us to begin. Mary steps forward until the deacons are only a couple of feet before her on the couch. Our parents are on the loveseat to her left. "Isaiah 2:10," Mary says. *"Enter into the rock and hide in the dust from before the terror of the Lord, and from the splendor of his majesty."* Her voice is loud and sure. I love hearing her recite scripture. I love everything about her. As she falls back into line I mentally review what I've memorized from the book of John: *"Beloved, if God so loved us, we also ought to love one another."* I plan to look right at Mary when I say it.

Tommy approaches the deacons and announces that he'll be reciting Psalm 137:9. *"Blessed shall be he who takes your little ones,"* he says, *"and dashes him against the rock."* He steps back. The deacons stare at him for a moment, looking disturbed, perhaps because they don't understood that his nature, as my parents' sometimes say, casts a long shadow.

They understand Timmy's nature, though, his love of the-
atrics and flair, and they beam in anticipation as he tilts his
face toward the ceiling and raises his hands above his head.
"Revelation 21:1!" he bellows. "'*Then I saw an angel coming
down from heaven, holding in his hand the key to the bottomless
pit and a great chain. And he seized the dragon, that ancient serpent, who is the devil and Satan, and bound him for a thousand
years, and threw him into the pit, and shut it and sealed it over
him, so that he might not deceive the nations any longer, until the
thousand years were ended.*'" As the deacons and my parents
applaud, Timmy bows, one arm still raised.

Linda follows with a short quote from Philippians about
rejoicing in the Lord, and now it's my turn. I move forward.
As I glance over my shoulder at Mary, she smiles. The words
in my head vanish, leaving hollow space.

"Jerry?" my father says.

"Yes, sir?"

"Are you ready?"

"Yes, sir."

"Well, go ahead then. What will you be reciting?"

I glance back at Mary. She nods, urging me to speak, but
my mind is still blank. I look at the deacons. They nod too.
A flash of memory enables me to blurt out that my scripture
is from the book of John, but I can't recall the chapter and
verse, so I mumble 2:21, the month and day of my birth. I
look at Mary again and try to speak like an apostle. "I say
unto thee we must loveth one another for thou is most lovely
and the Lord hath thus commanded this love." Heat engulfs
my face as my brothers laugh. Mary places her hand on her
heart and looks, as I feel, on the verge of tears. I lower my
gaze and move back into line. Bubba has developed a slight
stutter and doesn't like to recite scripture, so he concludes

our performance with a very brief Proverb about aiding the poor.

The next night we perform again, only without an audience, without the Bible and, at times, without God. We are the Jackson 5, and we sing their songs and dance their dances and get into heated arguments about which of us is Michael. At one point our father comes from his bedroom and threatens to break our records, so we lower our voices and argue some more. We finally agree to take turns being Michael, and when I'm him, I serenade Mary without forgetting the words to "I'll Be There," because it's easier to be a pop star than an apostle.

Our ministers know this too. That's why they preach so hard against popular music, sometimes singling out offensive artists and bands by name, like the Ohio Players and the Rolling Stones, but our parents let us listen to them anyway, as long as our homework is done and the volume is low. And sometimes they listen too. They especially like the Jackson 5 because, even though they haven't been chosen, they're God-fearing Christians who sing wholesome songs of love that you can repeat to your older sister. And so while our model of perfection will always be Jesus of Nazareth, the Jacksons of Gary are close behind, so close that one Saturday morning we're allowed to break the Sabbath to watch their new cartoon show, and a couple of times a week, after Bible study, we get to push the living room furniture aside to practice their dance routine.

In December we're ready for our first show. Our parents are the audience. Their blindness works in our favor as we bump into each other and move so out of synch that it appears to be on purpose. Midway through the act our father sends for another beer, his sixth, and after his seventh no one is surprised when he rises to join the band. He stumbles into the center of the room, and with Linda and Mary holding his arms, we go through our routine, no worse for the addition of a blind man three sheets to the wind. Then our mother gives in to our calls for her to join the band too, and with Bubba and me leading her, we dance and sing for another hour, pausing only to change the records, or when our laughter steals our breath so that all we can do is drop to our knees, clutch our sides, and wait for it to return.

Winkle returns in June. This time a sighted white woman drops him off and says she'll be back for him in two hours. Since two hours isn't long enough to teach him our song and dance routine, Bubba and I take him to meet Paul. Paul doesn't really want to play with him, though, because he knows the story of Winkle's death and resurrection, so Bubba and I take him to the park to push him on the swings.

After Winkle's gone we're told to forget him again, but this time the forgetting isn't aided by a new puppy. Instead, in November, all we get is another baby brother. We name this one André. André is only six days old, so tiny and frail that I'm afraid he'll break when I hold him. But I'm more afraid of someone taking him, like they've taken the others, and like they keep taking Winkle. I worry about this for three months. Then they take Pepper. He attacked André one day while he slept, mauling his right index finger so severely that it required God and a surgeon to save it. By the time André came home from the hospital, a whole week later, our beloved dog was gone.

My parents aren't sure we should get another one. They worry that André might be bitten again. And besides, they say, there is always a question of what to do with Pepper when we leave for the Place of Safety. It isn't clear that pets can go.

But something else isn't clear, at least not to me. Why do we keep getting foster children when we've entered the Last Days? Will the children be returned to the foster home before we leave, or will we take them with us, even though they aren't really ours to take? Are my parents trying to grow our family now since that won't be possible in the Kingdom of Heaven? Or maybe they don't believe in the Kingdom of Heaven after all. Maybe they are planning to leave the church, and, for now, they're only going through the motions.

These are complicated thoughts, and after a week I re-place them with a simple one that doesn't keep me up at night. When my parents chose to bring in foster children, I decide, they didn't consider the Place of Safety at all. They just love babies. I love them too. And I think, of all the ones we've had so far, André is my favorite. He doesn't cry much and he sleeps through the night. He sleeps a lot during the day too. I stand over his crib and watch him for long peri-ods, and when his body trembles I put a finger against his palm and let his tiny hand curl around it. And even though I know the trembling has something to do with his mother using drugs, I am certain, as his grip tightens, it has more to do with her giving him away.

It's early Sunday morning and Charlie Pride sings from the radio we keep on the kitchen counter. My mother stands at the sink humming quietly while washing the previous night's dishes. The ones she's finished are spread on the counter to her right, drying on two hand towels. An enormous pile waits on her left. For as long as I can remember our father's been saving to buy her a dishwasher, though he scolded me when I offered toward its purchase a quarter secretly withheld from the tithing pail.

When the song ends I enter the room and ask what's for breakfast. "Pancakes," she responds, her back to me. She dries her hands on her apron before walking to the refrigerator and taking out the carton of eggs. I can see her face now. She's not wearing her dark glasses. Without them she looks unnatural, and I know she feels this way too from how she keeps turning her head away from me. She probably thinks I'll stare at the grayish remains of her eyes, but I don't like doing that. I don't like staring at my father's eyes either, even though his appear normal. When I speak with my parents, I try to focus on their hair or their mouth or their nose, and in this way they aren't blind at all. They're just my parents. But when Jesus returns and gives them new eyes, I'll stare into them all the time.

I often wonder what my mother's will look like. The rest of ours are brown, so I hope hers will be too, but it'll be okay if they're violet like the one I saw a few years ago in her dresser. She asked me to get her a pair of nylons, and after I mistakenly opened the bottom instead of the middle drawer, I noticed the velvet, black case tucked in a nest of blouses and scarves. I thought it would contain a ring or a bracelet, but when I looked inside, I was surprised to see the inside looking back. My mother called, asking what was taking so long. I closed the case and returned it. A day later, when I went to examine the eye more closely, it was gone.

"Did you sleep well?"

"Yes," I say as I sit at the table.

"How about Mr. Teddy?"

The question irks me. I haven't slept with Mr. Teddy since I turned ten last month in February, entering, according to Paul, who's two months my senior, the realm of manhood. But if ten means being a man, so far it's fallen short of his reviews. My voice is still high, and I haven't gotten significantly taller or faster. While I wait to change I've taken the proactive step of banishing Mr. Teddy to the closet. I let him out only to wrestle when Bubba isn't in the mood or to act out an important comic book scene. At night I think of him as a fallen angel, bound for a thousand years in the pit of darkness. "No," I say, "I'm pretty certain Mr. Teddy didn't sleep well."

"Oh? Why not?"

"He's in the pit of darkness."

"The pit of darkness? What for?"

"For practicing integration," I say—an impulsive response, born from an unconscious need to know if this will be our fate as well—and I instantly realize I'm in trouble. I wouldn't have mentioned integration unless I'd been listening at their door.

That wasn't my plan. My plan was to go into the living room to watch television, but it changed when I neared their room and heard their muffled voices. I kneeled and put my ear against the door's gap; they were discussing what had come up last night at dinner. Mary had said a lot of homes in the neighborhood were for sale, four on our block alone. Our father explained that low interest rates had created an unstable housing market, but now he spoke of something sinister. Whites were leaving, he said, to avoid living near blacks.

I was surprised to hear my parents talking about race. They rarely do, even when we visit my mother's sister, Aunt Bernice, who talks about it all the time. Before we moved here, it was she who had warned us that our white neighbors would give us trouble. With only two years remaining before we were supposed to leave for the Place of Safety, I guess my parents felt that if there were any trouble, we wouldn't have to endure it for long.

There was no trouble. I wonder if my parents felt it was safe then to turn their attention from the judgment of our neighbors to the judgment of God, who was no more in favor of our move than Aunt Bernice, and for the same reason. They are both segregationists.

Mr. Armstrong is too. He told us Jesus is as well, as were Adam and Eve, but Eve's ovaries carried genes that could turn skin either brown or yellow. That was okay, until the colors mixed, sometimes to make new colors, sometimes to make war. Now we have a big mess on our hands, as the last decade of race riots prove, as does any American history book, especially ones with photos, because they're sure to have images of Negroes hanging from trees. Mr. Armstrong said his heart aches for those Negroes, just as much as it aches for the white folks who had to put them there. When he started Ambassador College in 1947, he must have wanted to avoid aching for anyone, because it was for whites only. In 1964 he finally allowed blacks in, but they had to be married; and seven years later, when he let single blacks enroll, there had to be a female for every male, in case they wanted to date. These changes were good news for Timmy, who'd be perfect for Ambassador College, and once the path was cleared, he was sure to be accepted. All he had to do was continue to study his Bible and to promise to stay as far away as humanly possible from white female coeds.

Sometimes members of our congregation openly complain about the church's views on race. They question if it is true that the Kingdom of Heaven will be segregated, and that eventually all black Chosen Ones will be sent back to Africa to help God rule there. These complaints aren't new, which is why Mr. Armstrong devoted a whole issue of *The Plain Truth* to the subject of race, with particular emphasis on what could be done to make the lives of Negroes better. He published it in 1963, and eleven years later we still have the issue in our home, resting on the coffee table next to the dish of stale peppermint candy.

I've thumbed through it many times, so I know social fellowship between the races is against God's law, and violating that law was why he caused the Great Flood, killing all but Noah and his family. And I know the main problem with integration is that it leads to intermarriage, which leads to a polluted bloodstream, which could make God's sacrifice of his only son a big mistake, because we'll all be damned. We're close to being damned already. Our only hope is to trust that God knew what he was doing when he ordained not only segregation but also white supremacy, a point we were to deduce from the fact that whites inherited the race of Jesus. But for being the descendants of slaves, Mr. Armstrong added, blacks have made out pretty well, so the best way for us to improve our lives is to stop counting our injustices and start counting our Cadillacs and televisions. And we definitely should ignore civil rights activists, because they speak not with the voice of God, but with the voice of Satan.

As I tiptoed from my parents' bedroom door, I wondered how Satan convinced them to move here. Did he lure them to South Shore with promises of good schools and low crime? Did he come to them as they slept, filling their formless dreams with notions of a multiracial community? What would he say to them now that our white neighbors were leaving? And would they listen this time too? I couldn't blame them if they did. It's hard not to listen when Satan speaks. I listened to him this morning. *Go to your sisters' room*, he told me, and I climbed down from my bed, the sound of my brothers' snores fading as I crossed the hall.

Like the boys' room, the girls' has two windows. Theirs face the street and are good places to see who is outside on Saturday mornings ready to laugh at us as we leave for church. A nightstand with two drawers sits in front of the windows. The top drawer is where Linda keeps her diary. I took it out and thumbed through it, but I had trouble understanding the words, because they were in cursive and the room was too dark. I put it back. Mary stirred, repositioning herself, her eyes still closed. She lay on the bed to my right. Linda was to my left. Behind me was their dresser. I headed there next.

I went through all the drawers and found nothing I wanted, other than the latest issue of *Jet Magazine* with Michael Jackson on the cover. I took it and went to the closet, at the rear of which is a small, sliding door that leads to a space four feet wide and four feet tall and runs the length of the house. Our parents use one end of it for storage. The other end is where my brothers and I keep our comic books. We have hundreds in our collection, some we haven't opened yet because we're saving them for the Place of Safety so we won't get bored reading the same old stories. I eased open the door a crack and slipped in the *Jet Magazine*. Then I went downstairs to watch TV, but I ended up listening to Satan again, who was telling me to listen to my parents.

"Integration?" my mother says to me. "And how was Mr. Teddy practicing integration?"

"No, not, not practicing *integration*," I stammer. "For practicing . . . fornication." I don't know what *fornication* means, but based on how tension fills the congregation when our ministers preach against it, and based on how tension is filling the kitchen now, I know I've accused Mr. Teddy of a very bad thing. It's out of respect for this badness, I hope, and not because of my blunder, that my mother doesn't speak or move for a long time. When she finally does it's to excuse herself and go to her room. I hear her say something to my father. I can't make it out, but I know it's about me. My palms turn clammy as I realize I'll have to admit that Satan brought me to their door like he brought them to live with white people.

But when my mother returns she doesn't send me to my father. She pauses by my chair, extends her hand, finds my shoulder for a gentle squeeze, and then asks how many pancakes I want. She's wearing her dark glasses now. In the lenses, I see myself smile and say, "Two."

The bell sends our classmates tripping over each other to reach the door. Bubba and I stay behind to speak with Mr. Smith, the fourth grade English teacher. He's erasing the board. I clear my throat to get his attention. When he turns, I hand him our mother's typed note explaining our need to miss school tomorrow because of Passover. He reads it before asking what we've been asked by all our previous teachers when we handed them this note. "Are you Jews?"

I answered incorrectly only once. We were in kindergarten then, and our teacher was Mrs. Giordani, a woman about whom I had mixed feelings. On the one hand, she was very pretty and I enjoyed looking at her, but on the other hand, she wore makeup and was therefore a prostitute. I shouldn't have enjoyed looking at a prostitute, I knew, but it was impossible to turn away from her sparkling, hazel eyes. I remember how they'd widened as she read our mother's note and then narrowed when she asked us about being Jews. I looked at Bubba. He hunched his shoulders. I looked back at Mrs. Giordani. "Yes," I said. "We're Jews."

I enjoyed being a Jew. The word was easy to pronounce, and when I said it, people responded with a slow nod, like Mrs. Giordani, instead of the double takes I got when I said I was a Chosen One. That confused people. Then they'd ask me questions that sometimes I had no memorized answers for. I never got questions about being a Jew. People seemed to know all they needed to know about them, and Sally Huxley, who lay next to me during naptime, even knew that one of them was Sammy Davis Jr. "And he's Afro-American," she pointed out, "such as yourself."

"How do you know he's a Jew?" I asked.

"I've seen pictures of him wearing one of those little round hats."

I didn't have a little round hat. Neither did anyone in my family or in our congregation. Mr. Armstrong didn't wear one either. "Do all Jews wear these little round hats?" I asked.

"How the heck would *I* know?" she said. "*You're* the Jew."

After school I put the question of the little round hats to Timmy. He was in the dining room studying one of his chess books. He closed it after marking his place. "We don't wear little round hats like other Jews," he said, "because we're not Jews."

"We're not?"

"No, Jerry. Jews are descendants of Judah. We're descendants of David. We're *Israelites*. That means, unlike Jews, we accept Christ as our Lord and Savior. Don't you know that?"

I wasn't sure what I knew. There was a lot to memorize, and I couldn't keep it all straight.

"Well," he continued, "you *do* know that we're God's Chosen Ones?"

That much was clear.

"And do you know what happens to Chosen Ones when they pretend to be something else?"

"God gets angry?"

"Correct. And do you want to know what he does then?"

"No, thank you," I said, backing away. I went to read a comic book, glad to have the matter of the little round hats resolved, as well as my identity. I wasn't a Jew. I wasn't very smart either. Certainly not as smart as Timmy. My parents said he had a special ability to take photographs with his mind and view them later like a slideshow. That's why the Bible passages he recited for the deacons were always the longest. And sometimes, just for fun, he memorized passages on his own and recited them during dinner. On the evening I asked about the little round hats, after our father had blessed the meal, Timmy announced that he'd memorized not one passage, but two.

He usually focused on the book of Revelation, like our ministers, so Bubba and I tried not to listen to him either. But when he grinned at me as he rose from his chair, I had a suspicion this recital would hold special relevance. "John 3:18," he began. "*Whoever believes in him is not condemned, but whoever does not believe is condemned already, because he has not believed in the name of the only Son of God.*" I was reaching for my scar when he announced that his second passage was from the book of Ezekiel. "*When I snuff you out, I will cover the heavens and darken their stars; I will cover the sun with a cloud, and the moon will not give its light.*"

I excused myself and went to my room. My mother joined me a short while later. I had already changed into my pajamas and gotten into bed. I told her I wasn't feeling well. She rested the back of her hand on my forehead. Finding no fever, she asked me if anything was wrong at school, and I didn't see how I could avoid making matters worse without confessing I'd spent the last three days as a Jew. "Am I condemned?" I asked.

"No, sweetie," she said.

"Will I be snuffed out?"

"You won't be snuffed out either. I'll send your teacher another note tomorrow."

She did, explaining that we belonged to the Worldwide Church of God, a Christian denomination. I memorized these words and repeated them each year to our teachers, as I do now with Mr. Smith. Then I'm the one doing the double take when he says he celebrates Passover too.

"I'm Jewish," he tells us. "But for us, Passover begins this Saturday. And yours starts Friday?"

I nod.

"How do you observe it?"

"We go to church and watch people wash feet," Bubba says. "But first we have to clean our house of leaven. We have to keep it out for a whole week."

"Ah," he says, smiling, "the *chametz*."

Bubba and I exchange a look.

"*Chametz*," he repeats. "That's Hebrew for foods that contain leaven."

"Do you have to get rid of it too?"

"Oh, yes. I did when I was younger, anyway. And let me tell you," he says, winking, "it was a *pain*."

"Why don't you still get rid of it?" Bubba asks.

"I should, I suppose. I'm not as devout as I used to be." He pauses and adds with a whisper, "Promise not to tell my parents."

We promise, even though we don't know his parents. And before this moment, we didn't know anyone outside our church who observed Passover and had to get rid of leaven. I wonder if Mr. Smith knows about the Tribulation. Bubba reads my mind and asks, "You know the world is ending, right?"

Now he does a double take. "Is that what your church believes?"

Bubba nods. "It was supposed to happen two years ago but it's been delayed."

"Until?"

I say probably next year.

"I see," he says. "I see."

But he doesn't see. I can tell. He doesn't believe in the Tribulation and he probably thinks we're strange. I lift my book bag from the floor and hoist it over my shoulder. Bubba grabs his. As we walk toward the door, Mr. Smith wishes us a happy Passover. I stop and face him. "Mr. Smith?"

"Yes?"

"If you're a Jew, why aren't you wearing a little round hat?"

"The little round hats are called yarmulkes."

"Why aren't you wearing one?"

"Not all Jews do," he says.

And there's my answer.

W e've been removing leaven for two days and I'm worried we won't finish in time, especially with the kitchen. My mother is taking every box and can from the cupboard, handing them to Tommy to read the ingredients. If she says it's okay, he gives it back and she returns it to the shelf. If it's not okay, he places it into the garbage bag at his feet. Every time I check on them, they seem to be standing at the same place examining the same things. At 1:30 p.m., with fewer than four hours remaining, I warn them if they don't go faster, God will smite us.

Tommy looks at me. "Smite?"

I'm learning the proper way to speak like an apostle, thanks to Timmy. He said *smite* was a good word to use. This is my first time taking it for a test drive, and I'm pleased to see I've run over my seventeen-year-old brother. "Yes," I say. "Smite. It means to be crushed like a bug."

"I know what *smite* means, Einstein."

"Have you finished checking your clothes?" my mother asks.

"I finished yesterday."

"You've checked *all* your pants' pockets?"

"Yes, ma'am."

"How about your book bag, like I told you to do earlier?"

"Continue thy Lord's good work," I say as I back out the door.

Before cleaning out my book bag, I go upstairs to find Timmy. He's finished vacuuming and is returning the furniture he moved. "Give me a hand," he says, motioning toward the dresser. It's crowded with a dozen trophies he won as captain of his high school's chess team; we nudge it by inches until it comes to rest against the wall beneath two posters of Bobby Fischer and a copy of our sacred calendar. The calendar is confusing because it's based on the Old Testament, so the first month is April instead of January. After I accidentally became a Jew, Timmy took me on as his private pupil. Sometimes he names one of our seven annual festivals, and I have to tell him which month we celebrate it. Right now he's asking me the purpose of Passover. This is simple. Passover is our most important observance and it's followed by the Feast of Unleavened Bread, which isn't exactly my idea of a feast, because for seven days we can't eat things like cookies, cake, biscuits, or Twinkies. And it's not only a sin for leaven to be in our bodies; it's a sin for it to be in our lives. "Why couldn't it be called something else?" I ask. "Like the Feast of No Lima Beans?"

"Lima beans are definitely vile," Timmy responds. "But that's the problem. It would be too easy not to eat them. To prove your loyalty to God, the test has to be difficult." Excited now by the opportunity to give a lecture, he opens his ever-handy Bible and reads scriptures about leaven and Egypt and Moses, but my desire to learn fails to match his desire to teach. My mind wanders to a funny episode of *The Three Stooges*.

Timmy closes his Bible, the lecture done. He seems pleased to see me smiling. He smiles back. "Is it not a blessed thing to study the righteous words of our Lord?" he asks.

"Verily, verily, I say unto thee."

"Cool," he says, grinning. "You've been practicing."

"As thou instructed."

He puts his arm around my shoulder. "Come on, devoted pupil. Let us depart this wretched wilderness of our bedroom and assist our kin in thy pursuits to cast out leaven from our lair."

We head to the den, where Bubba and Linda are cleaning out their book bags, but first I pop my head into the kitchen to check on my mother and Tommy's progress. "How goeth thou's labor?"

"Will you *stop* talking like that?" Tommy snaps.

"Oh, leave him alone," my mother says, laughing. "He's just being silly."

"He's being a retard, like Timmy." He pulls the drawstring tight on his garbage bag. All the cabinet drawers are closed and my mother is washing her hands.

"Are you finished?" I ask.

They are. I look at my watch and see that there are still two hours before the Sabbath and the start of Passover. Technically, we have a little more than twenty-four hours to finish de-leavening, but our weekly trash pickup is early the next morning and we need to get our captured leaven off our property. For the next two hours, everyone pitches in to hunt down crumbs in likely and unlikely places: under the stove; in the toaster; on closet shelves; inside mittens; between the pages of books; in the garage; and under the welcome mat outside our front door. When we finish, Tommy carries the garbage bags to our trashcans in the alley. Then we get ready for the Passover service.

The cars arrive at dusk, just as some kids from our block are walking by. Later, they'll ask Bubba and me where we'd gone, why were we so dressed up, why the Bibles, why the serious expressions, why were our parents carrying plastic buckets, and why, when they called to us to say hello, we didn't respond. To avoid these questions, I try to stall leaving the house by saying I forgot my Bible. Linda points out that it's in my hand.

Tommy, our mother, Mary, with André bundled in her arms, go to the lead car. It's owned by Mr. Martin, a middle-aged parishioner who likes to give us butterscotch candy. The rest of us ride with an elderly couple named Mr. and Mrs. St. Claire. They drive a station wagon with a third row that faces backward. Bubba and I love riding there, but Linda and Timmy do as well, so our parents make us alternate; this time Bubba and I are in luck. We swing open the long rear door and climb inside while Timmy, Linda, and our father sit in the middle row. Mr. St. Claire always drives and his wife always sits next to him explaining how. But she won't explain how tonight, because, with the exception of the sermon, speaking during Passover is discouraged. The occasion is too solemn for words.

We've been silent for the last hour, and we're silent on the drive to the service. We walk toward the school's entrance without saying a word, and when we reach the deacon, who sometimes asks my siblings and me how we're doing in our studies and exchanges small talk with our parents, he simply looks beyond us as he holds open the door.

Instead of going to the auditorium, we go to a large class-room on the second floor. All the desks have been pushed against the wall, and the chairs are arranged in two groups in the center of the room; half designated for the men, half for the women. Much of the congregation is already here, probably well over a hundred people. The adults have placed their buckets on the floor before their chairs and now sit in quiet meditation while the children look around the room, some of them, like Bubba and me, making a game of not speaking by rapidly blinking their eyes, a kind of Morse Code. I'm not sure what Bubba's blinks are saying, but mine are telling him to look at Mr. Gills, who's already removed his shoes and socks, exposing what are less recognizable as feet than goat hooves.

Once everyone is seated, the deacons take two of the water pitchers from a seminar table and begin filling the buckets. When each bucket contains about an inch of water, the minister says a prayer and then all the adults remove their footwear. Some members approach others and, still silent, the washing begins. This is a sign of humility, as Christ humbled himself before his followers, and I wonder if he had a test of will such as the one presented to the man paired with Mr. Gills. My father's feet are no prizewinners either, and after a quick survey of this side of the room, I'm repulsed enough to violate the gender code. I reach my mother's side as someone gently cups her heels and places her feet into her bucket of water. A moment later, she and the woman exchange places.

After all the feet have been washed, everyone receives a cup of grape juice, which symbolizes wine, which in turn symbolizes Christ's blood. Then we are given a piece of flat-bread, as the Israelites took during their flight from Pharaoh's army, so desperate they were to escape that they didn't have time for the baking bread to rise. This is the subject of the minister's sermon. And I don't mind listening to it, because I like the story of how God freed the Israelites from slavery. I don't even mind when the minister says *we* are slaves, true modern-day Israelites, because he reminds us that our freedom is near. At any moment the world will fall to anarchy and pestilence, and the Chosen Ones will leave for the Place of Safety. During the silence of the drive home, I close my eyes and picture my family in a caravan of camels, moving sluggishly across moonlit dunes.

I t's the Night to Be Much Observed, and we're commemorating the Israelites' departure from Egypt. Dinner is finished and now our host, Mrs. Devin, is talking up her brownies. The brownies aren't brown but yellow, which disqualifies them as edible even before she explains that they were made without chocolate or sugar, due to her husband's cocoa allergy and her diabetes. And of course they were made without leaven; all the wives in the four families here contributed dishes without leaven, which wasn't an issue for the things that shouldn't have contained it, like the macaroni and cheese and the potato salad, but the baked confections presented challenges that weren't overcome. The treats are arranged in the center of the table; cookies, cakes, pies, and "brownies" that are barely thicker than the plates holding them, as if they were prepared with a hot iron rather than an oven. For several minutes, the ten children who are present smell, nudge, poke, and view the desserts from various angles, then abandon them entirely in favor of playing with the Devin's two puppies.

We toss them tennis balls in the basement for a while, and then someone suggests we take turns lying on the floor and having the puppies dropped on our bellies. Linda goes first and we are in hysterics as the puppies tumble off her before climbing up again, stumbling along her legs, falling off, climbing back up, now bouncing on her torso. Bubba goes next, then a five-year-old girl, then two of the teenagers before it's finally my turn. At first I'm enjoying myself, but when one of the puppies catches me on the face with a nail, I have a flashback of Milo's teeth ripping into my flesh. I send the puppies into a free-fall as I scramble to my feet, yelling that I'm being bitten.

"Bitten?" one of the kids says. "They're not *biting* you! They're *puppies!*"

Timmy tells them about what had happened with Milo, adding that the fault was mine for celebrating Christmas.

I dispute this. *"Mommy* let us go to Paul's."

"But *you* were bitten," he says, "which means *you* sinned." He points to my scar. The kids lean toward me and nod like I'm an art exhibit.

A girl Timmy's age says, *"'Salvation and glory and power belong to our God, for his judgments are true and just.'"*

Timmy smiles at her. "Revelation?"

"Chapter nineteen," she says. "Verse one."

"Very impressive."

He grins and she blushes, and before their flirting makes us all nauseated, the game resumes. I don't want to play anymore, but it's impossible to stay afraid of the puppies. Soon I'm taking turns having them trample me like everyone else. I don't even panic when I'm scratched on the face again.

Bubba and I say nothing to our father about the puppies during the ride home. Once home we don't mention them as he drinks a half dozen beers, or when the Chicago Bulls' game ends and he changes the radio station to bluegrass, or when he goes from tapping his fingers on his thigh to humming off tune. But as soon as he breaks into song, we make our move.

"Another *puppy?*" he replies. Then he finishes the chorus. This is a good sign. He's decisive when his answer is no.

"Actually," I say. "Two puppies."

"*Two* puppies!" he repeats. He sings some more. When the song ends, he says if we get him another beer, we can have *three* puppies.

Bubba and I fly to the kitchen. Our mother's sweeping but stops to ask us what all the commotion is about. We tell her we're getting three puppies. I snatch open the refrigerator door and Bubba grabs a beer. He keeps it as steady as possible while we run back. After our father pries open the can, he fills his empty glass. Then, as always, he offers Bubba and me a swallow, which we always accept. As we complete the ritual our mother joins us.

"Puppies?" she says. "Did you promise them puppies?"

Our father reaches for the radio and lowers the volume. "I said I'd think about it."

I correct him. "You said we could *have* them."

Our mother corrects me. "No one's getting any puppies."

Bubba and I look to her and then back to our father, who says she's right. No puppies. This time he doesn't mention André being bitten. He mentions how Mr. Armstrong's work paving the way for Christ's return is nearly complete, but it might fall short, he's informed us, unless he receives some extra tithes.

Paying extra tithes will be hard on my parents. Despite the quarters I once waved over the collection pail, we are, in fact, poor. If we weren't receiving welfare to supplement our father's salary, we couldn't get by. Yet our parents never fail to respond to Mr. Armstrong's requests for extra tithes, even if it means our house is cold in winter, we wear clothes from Goodwill, eat government-provided peanut butter and cheese, and drink transparent milk made from powder and water. And now, with days, weeks, and possibly months of hiding in our basement with only canned foods to eat, which is already a scenario I'm not looking forward to, there won't be any puppies to keep us company.

I try not to let this upset me. I try not to be upset about anything that happens as a result of our faith. When these negative impulses are upon me, I remind myself how lucky I am to be chosen, handpicked by God to do his will in exchange for eternal life. Eternal life is a good long while, I tell myself, which means I'll be able to visit every country on our globe as often as I want, and I'll be able to do it without the aid of a private jet or my parents' money. And instead of being elderly and possibly senile like Mr. Armstrong, I'll always be young, always just a boy, unaffected by time.

I think about this for several minutes as Bubba and I sit silently in the living room. When I feel a little better, I try to strike up a conversation about having lightning bolts, in an effort to lift his spirits. But it's no use. He doesn't want to talk about lightning bolts. He wants to sulk. I give up resisting after a while and join him.

The payment for our sulking comes due Monday morning, when God sends Sara Robinson to school with cupcakes. She places a whole bin full of them on Mr. Smith's desk and stands in front of the blackboard grinning and soaking up her instant celebrity. While telling us she's ten years old to-day, she tucks a strand of blonde hair behind her ear, catch-ing the string of her birthday hat and causing it to rest at an odd angle. A few kids see this as high comedy and burst into laughter. After order has been restored in the classroom and to Sara's appearance, Mr. Smith leads the singing of "Happy Birthday." Bubba and I can't celebrate birthdays, so we don't sing. And because we can't eat leavened foods this week, we won't be having any of those cupcakes either.

When the song is finished, Sara picks up the bin and announces she has four flavors from which to choose: vanilla, chocolate, strawberry, and *Neapolitan*. I've never heard of Neapolitan-flavored cupcakes, and this strikes me as an important advancement in the field of treats. I only wish I wasn't learning of it when I can't try one. I wish too that when Sara paused by the side of my desk, Mr. Smith didn't say, loud enough for the whole class to hear, that the Walker twins can't eat cupcakes this week on account of our religion.

This is more high comedy. I add Mr. Smith and everyone who laughs to my list of people I won't be pulling from the lake of fire. Some of the kids don't laugh but instead look at Bubba and me with pity, which is worse than laughing, so I put them on the list too. And then there are the kids who neither laugh nor pity us; they only want to know more about a religion that doesn't allow cupcakes. They put their questions to Bubba and me during recess. We explain that we don't celebrate birthdays because we don't celebrate Christ's.

"Why not?" a girl asks.

I say, "Because we don't know when it is."

"Actually," she responds, "it's December twenty-fifth."

Bubba tells her that date isn't in scripture.

"So?" she says. "What does scripture have to do with it?"

"I just want to know about the cupcakes," says a boy. "Where do they fit in?"

"That's easy," answers another. "The cupcake is the body of Christ."

I shake my head. "We don't believe Christ's body is a cupcake."

"*God* is the cupcake?"

Bubba says no.

"So why can't you eat one?"

"Because they're Jews," someone says.

"I know a Jew," a girl states, "and she eats plenty of cupcakes."

"They're *Afro*-Jews."

I say we're not Afro-Jews.

"They're *Jehovah's* Jews."

"We're not Jehovah's Jews either," Bubba responds.

"So whose Jews are you?"

"We're *no one's* Jews," I snap.

"Then what's your religion?"

"*It doesn't matter!*" I yell. "We just *can't* eat the stupid cupcakes! *Okay? We just can't!*" I turn and head toward the far end of the playground. Bubba tries to follow me, but I tell him to leave me alone. When I reach the chain-link fence that surrounds the lot, I lower myself to the gravel, my arms clutching my knees. I stay here until the bell rings.

At lunchtime Bubba and I sit by ourselves in the cafeteria. We could sit with the other kids, but neither of us is in the mood to answer more questions, and there are always questions when we are sent to school with matzo and cheese sandwiches. As we slowly remove them from our lunchboxes, I can sense the stares coming from all directions, and at this moment I realize I'll be stared at not only for the rest of the lunch period but for the rest of my life. Stared at when I go to church on Saturday; stared at when I mention the Tribulation and the lake of fire; stared at when I have to explain why I don't celebrate pagan holidays; stared at when I give teachers my mother's notes; and stared at, lately, when I stand before the mirror trying to identify the thing that makes me special, a boy worthy of eternal life in God's Kingdom of Heaven, but all I ever see is my plain, ordinary face, forever altered now by an ugly scar.

Tonight, after brushing my teeth, I stare into the mirror again, only this time I dare to voice the thought that crept into my mind during recess and frightened me even more than our ministers' sermons. "I wish I hadn't been chosen," I whisper. "I wish I was just a normal boy."

The Feast of Pentecost is our holy day that says the Lord is a giant farmer and we'll be the first fruits of his harvest. This morning our head minster preaches for a full hour about first fruits, which makes me wish I hadn't slept in and missed breakfast. Our father must have gotten up very early for breakfast, because he sleeps for the entire second half of the sermon. When he wakes he's in a good mood, which he credits to the minister's strong performance, and during the drive home he keeps saying how inspiring the message was. Once we arrive, he even wants us to describe our favorite parts. We never get the chance, though. As soon as he walks into the living room, he collapses in convulsions.

Our mother throws herself on top of him and begins working her fingers between his clenched teeth, offering them for sacrifice to spare his tongue. His pills are in the medicine cabinet, she yells, and after Mary gets them, our mother presses one between our father's lips, now covered with blood we'll later learn isn't his. Tommy calls 911, Bubba and I join Linda and Mary in prayer, Timmy recites scripture, and André, because he's too young to do anything else, throws a tantrum. This is the scene that greets the paramedics. They look more shaken than we do.

Three of my mother's fingers are severely gouged. The
paramedics say they're at risk of becoming infected. They
want to take her to the ER. But she refuses to let them,
which I don't understand. Would it be a sin for her to go
to the hospital this time? Is God available to heal her from
home? And what about my father? The medicine has taken
effect and he's conscious, able to stand with the paramedics'
assistance and to object to being placed on the gurney. Is
he concerned about sinning too, even though he's already
sinned by taking the medicine? Now that I think about it,
how did he get the medicine in the first place? And if our father *can* take medicine, why do Bubba and I have to bring a
note to school every year explaining that our religion forbids
us from receiving vaccinations?

The paramedics wheel our father out the door. I hurry
to the picture window, less to witness his departure than to
see what witnesses there are. The coast is clear. But I know
that doesn't necessarily mean anything. So I'm not surprised
a short while later when Paul's father rings our bell. By the
time our mother finishes explaining what happened, other
neighbors have drifted from their homes and cluster together
facing ours. They move forward as Paul's father approaches.

The next day, when Bubba and I take our bicycles out
for a ride, the three boys who join us are well versed in one
chapter of our father's story: he's an epileptic. Now they want
another chapter, the one that explains his blindness beyond
what we've told them, which is only that he fell.

My father was twelve and living in a three-story brown-
stone. A light rain had left the brick porch steps slick, and as
my father ran down them, his feet swept upward; he reached
his hands back to break his fall, but his head hit first. A lump

grew behind his right ear that he knew to treat with ice, but he didn't know how to stop the waves of pain that crashed against his temple. They finally ceased on their own after two weeks, only to be replaced by vertigo. The dizzy spells were scary, but nothing like the fear he soon experienced about his vision. At first he only had trouble focusing on objects in the far distance, but the far distance slowly grew near, until one morning everything beyond a foot of his nose was a blur. His grandmother watched him pat the kitchen floor one morning, unable to find the fork he'd accidentally knocked from the table, and burst into tears.

The emergency room physician explained that blood clots had formed on my father's occipital lobes, compromising his sight. A good surgeon could restore his vision, he was told. But the one who tried was not good. Once the mishandled scalpel had destroyed the little sight that remained, my father was wheeled from the operating room with a metal plate in his skull and a life expectancy of one more year. The surgeon who predicted his life expectancy was not good either.

I finish my father's story, and for a while the boys do nothing other than shake their heads. We are sitting on a neighbor's freshly mowed lawn, the loose blades sticking to our sweaty hands and legs. Our bicycles are in a tilted row along the walkway like Harley's outside a bar, and on the other side of the bicycles, where the lawn resumes, is one of a half-dozen For Sale signs that span the block. A couple of the signs have stickers slanted across their fronts that read SOLD. Almost all the white kids we once played with have already moved. In two months, Sean, Dave, and Dave's little brother John, the boys we're with now, will have too.

Sean reclines on his elbows and, staring toward the sky, says that something about my father's story doesn't add up. "I don't see how no one noticed he was losing his sight."

Bubba says, "He hid it."

Sean shakes his head. "You can't hide being blind."

"Well, he did."

"How?"

I say, "He stopped going out to play with his friends."

Sean sits upright, his arms circling his pale knees, his cobalt-blue eyes directed at me. "What about school?"

"School was out. It was summer."

"What about his family?"

"His mother wasn't alive," I explain. "He had two older brothers and a sister, but they weren't around much."

"His father didn't notice?"

His father was an alcoholic who only noticed his sobriety and ways to end it, but I lie and say he worked two jobs and was rarely home. Dave asks about his grandmother. I could mention her vision problems, the severe case of cataracts that plagued her for years, but I don't feel I need to offer this level of detail. I'm tired of explaining my own life as it is; I don't want to spend a lot of time on my father's. "I don't know," I say. "She just didn't notice."

"Didn't notice? He was *blind.*"

"And?"

"And? *And?* And he would have been bumping into furniture and walls and stuff, that's *and?*"

"He probably did at first," Bubba concedes.

A screech of wheels. We follow the sound to the street where a Buick idles only a couple of feet from where a black girl, one of our new neighbors, holds a beach ball. She pivots, runs toward a house and through an open gate leading to the backyard. The car creeps forward and we watch it silently until it turns the corner. The distraction probably would have ended the discussion, so I don't know why Bubba resumes it. "After he lost his sight," he says, "his seizures started."

"Does he have them a lot?" John asks.

"He used to. But now he has medicine that controls them."

"So why'd he have the seizure?"

"He forgot to take it."

"He should tie a piece of string on his finger," John offers, "to help him remember."

The gate snaps. The girl has returned. She's exchanged the beach ball for a jump rope and starts jumping as John asks about our mother's blindness.

When Bubba says it started with mucus, the boys look confused, as my grandparents must have while inspecting the condition of their newborn's left eye. It was probably a severe case of conjunctivitis, but in that rural Arkansas community in 1936 *conjunctivitis* wasn't a known word and the city doctors who knew it weren't trusted enough to visit. So an elderly neighbor offered a diagnosis of "Just needs to be kick started," and various remedies were set in motion, including drops of gasoline, a dusting of baking powder, cigar smoke, cigarette ashes, and even urine from a cow. By my mother's first birthday, her left eye was as dead as the community's faith in the medical profession. But her right eye was alive and served her well until she was nine. Then one day when she was feeling overburdened, her mother gave her the latest in a long list of chores, this one to change her infant brother's diaper, and my mother refused. She ran outside, glancing over her shoulder after clearing the yard to see if she was being chased, now swiveling her head back as an older brother moved his mule-drawn cart into her path. The two-by-four protruding from the cart could have hit her nose, or her chin, or her forehead, or even poked her arm or shoulder, but it landed square in her good eye, exactly as God intended.

Bubba finishes her story. I follow it with her warning. "Never disobey your parents," I say. "Never disobey your parents, or God will punish you." The boys are quiet again, each of them deep in thought, and I wonder if they're considering the image of a nine-year-old girl lying on the ground, clutching her sudden blindness, or reflecting on their own instances of disobedience and fearing for their sight.

Sean rises, says he has to go, that it's nearly time for dinner. After John and Dave agree, all three boys mount their bicycles and peddle away. So Bubba and I are left alone to contemplate the moral of our mother's story, as we often have before, and what comes to my mind this time is yesterday's Feast of Pentecost service, how our father slumped low in his chair, mouth ajar, chin on chest, and slept through half of the sermon. So I know that tying a piece of string to his finger wouldn't have prevented his seizure. This wasn't a matter of forgetfulness. This was a matter of vengeance. When God decides to punish you for wrongdoing, his aim is sure, and there's nothing you can do but accept the blow.

We've made it through the rest of the summer without our father having another seizure. Our mother's fingers didn't become infected. But there's still bad news. Mary is leaving. I knew she'd applied and been accepted to a number of colleges, but I never thought she'd actually go. Now it's the night before she does.

I've written her a good-bye letter. After I sign my name, I walk across the hall to her bedroom to sneak it into her suitcase while she's in the basement watching *Star Trek*, only I discover, after opening her door, that she's not in the basement watching *Star Trek*. She's sitting on the foot of her bed, facing the dresser's mirror as she combs her hair, topless.

She pauses when she sees me, takes in my gaping mouth and wide eyes as I wait to turn to stone. Only by God's grace am I able to stumble backward and into my room. Only Satan's mischievousness could have brought her to me. But instead of acknowledging what happened, she casually says hello, as if this is our first encounter of the day, an act of great compassion that enables me to ease my head from beneath the cover. She has a top on now, the white T-shirt with "Hoosiers" stitched across the front in crimson. All summer long it's been her second skin.

She sits next to me and ruffles my hair. "What's new?"

"Oh, not much," I say, yawning. "Just taking a little nap."

"In Bubba's bed?"

It was the first one I reached. "We're thinking of switching," I say. "Thought I'd try it out. What's new with you?"

"Big day for me tomorrow."

"Really?" I yawn again. "What's tomorrow?"

"You *know*." She ruffles my hair some more. "Thank you for the very sweet letter."

"What . . . what letter?"

"The one you dropped."

She's holding it up for me to see, I presume. My head is beneath the cover again.

"I like your penmanship."

I thank her.

"And I love the crayon color you used."

"Atomic Tangerine."

"Pardon?"

"The color's called Atomic Tangerine."

"Well, it's very pretty."

I appreciate the compliment. I also appreciate her suggestion that we be pen pals. I imagine composing stories about my life, maybe while imitating the calligraphy I've seen in fancy Bibles, and of actually receiving letters from her in return. It's a comforting thought, but I still don't want her to go. Besides, I know Corinthians tells us that the wisdom of the world is foolishness; that's why we're not supposed to watch the news or read newspapers or pay attention to politics or vote. So why we bother with school at all has long been a mystery to me. Is there a reason why, as gods, we'll need to know math and science? Or music, for that matter, as Mary is so obsessed with studying? From the moment she received the bulky acceptance folder from Indiana University, she's considered the course descriptions with the care Bubba and I once considered our superpowers, swapping one class for another and then back again, as if it really matters, as if she can actually complete her degree before the Tribulation obliterates her school. God commands us to prepare for heaven on earth, and here she is preparing for heaven *and* earth. It's sacrilegious, it seems to me. At the very least, it's a waste of time when there isn't any to waste.

Mr. Armstrong recently made this clear. All summer long, while I was monitoring the health of my parents, he was monitoring the health of the world. And what he saw wasn't good. In last month's newsletter, he described how governments were toppling like dominoes, places like Chile, Afghanistan, Bangkok, Cyprus, and Portugal, and then, only a few days ago, he added the United States to the list, citing the likely impeachment of President Nixon. All that we're witnessing, he said, was prophesied to occur right before The End. I hadn't thought Mary would have a chance to leave.

"Mary?"

"Yes?"

"If you had a choice, I mean, if *you* could choose, would you go to the Place of Safety with us or go to college?"

"I'll tell you if you come out from under there."

I poke my head out. The air is refreshing on my perspiring face.

"I'd choose to go with our family to the Place of Safety."

"Then why not just wait here and leave with us?"

"Because we don't know when it'll be."

"We know it'll be soon. Next year at the latest." I study her face, looking for evidence of the doubt I'm pretty certain her delayed response conveys. Her left eye twitches. "*What?*" I exclaim. "*You don't think it'll be soon?*"

"I think . . ." she begins, "I think only God knows whether or not it'll be soon."

"Mr. Armstrong knows. God *told* him."

"God can change his mind, you know. He has before."

"Do you want him to?"

She says, "Sometimes."

I'm not surprised by her answer. I noticed that during our last church service she eased a romance novel from her purse and slipped it between the pages of her Bible, desecrating the book of Luke. I've seen how she spends more and more time in the lobby talking to the teenaged boys who leer at her from the moment we arrive to the moment we leave. I've heard her argue with our parents about her curfew being too early and her phone privileges too few, about not being able to attend parties or to date or even to be alone with a suitor. And if my parents weren't blind, I would've heard them argue with her about her miniskirts and tube tops and lip gloss. No, she won't be disappointed if God changes his mind and Christ *never* returns. She'll be too busy being with some dumb boy.

"Why do you keep going under your sheet?"

"I'm cold."

"Cold? It has to be a hundred degrees in here." She rises and says she's going to watch *Star Trek*. "Want to come?"

"Mary?"

"Yes?"

"When Tribulation starts, how will you find us?"

"I'll find you."

"How?"

"God will show me where you are."

She leaves. I remain in Bubba's bed awhile longer, mentally composing my first pen-pal letter. I open it by stressing that when she joins us in the Place of Safety, she must come alone, and I remind myself to capitalize *alone* like Mr. Armstrong capitalizes words in his letters to emphasize what's at the heart of the matter. Some of his favorite words are *brink*, *little time*, *end*, and *prophesied*. I decide to use these too. "INSTEAD of waiting to JOIN US in the Place of Safety," I continue, "it is BETTER for you to COME HOME IMMEDIATELY, for it is PROPHESIED that families will be together at THE END and there is LITTLE TIME as we reach the BRINK !" Maybe I'll even mention the toppling of governments and what this foretells, and I'll remind her about the overthrow of Richard Nixon and of America's imminent collapse. I'll round off the letter with a speculation about the cause and effect of dating and boils. "So please COME HOME," I'll say in closing. "Your favorite brother. With LOVE."

The Feast of Trumpets is the fourth holy day of God's calendar year. It symbolizes when Christ will return to harvest the first fruits and establish the Kingdom on Earth. Our congregation always observes it with a daylong service in a special venue, usually downtown at the McCormick Place Convention Center, pausing midway for a picnic lunch on the manicured lawns along Lake Michigan's shore. Lunch is the best part. Bubba and I like sitting on the retaining wall near the water to watch the seagulls hover above the waves, and even though it's October, sometimes we can see sailboats, and, farther in the distance, barges and yachts. Once, when we were six, we asked our mother to join us. She took Bubba's arm and we headed to our favorite area, moving extra carefully because the grass was uneven—our mother was wearing heels—and Bubba and I were still learning how to be her eyes. As we reached the stone ledge, Bubba said, "We're here," but it didn't occur to either of us that she had no visual reference for what "here" was until she took one more step, and toppled over the edge.

Five feet below us, she lay face down on the jogging path—the only thing separating her from the deep, choppy water. Tommy and Timmy rushed over to help her up, then people came to us from all directions while Bubba and I cried, horrified by the thought of what happened and, worse, of what could've happened. Our mother's assurances to everyone that she wasn't hurt eventually calmed us. And ten minutes later, while we were eating our bologna and cheese sandwiches, Bubba and I even managed to giggle after she leaned toward us and whispered, "Thank goodness my wig stayed on. Now *that* was a miracle."

As Bubba and I sit on the retaining wall now, I'm hoping for another miracle, a more substantial one this time that results in our Lord and Savior stepping from his throne and onto the gentle waves. For eight weeks I've invested a lot of time in a fantasy of Christ and my sister Mary actually arriving simultaneously, her dashing from a taxi in front of the building while in back Christ mounts the shore. But in the end I know it won't happen. Mary wrote me to say she can't return, because she has an important exam, and Mr. Armstrong explained that Christ can't return, because our preparation for him isn't complete. And so instead of departing for the Place of Safety today with my family whole, I spend the endless church service nudging my father's side or tapping his knee whenever I hear him snore.

Ten days later Mary still hasn't come home to visit, so we have to observe the Day of Atonement without her. We sit at the dinner table, bow our heads in prayer, and at "Amen" I'm off to the races, burying my plate in more food than it should hold. I even consider scooping out a few lima beans when Tommy hands me the dish. "You may as well have some," he says, "if you and Bubba plan to rupture your abdominal walls."

Bubba's plate looks identical to mine: a mound of spaghetti, two fried chicken legs, sweet potatoes, mustard greens, and one and a half slices of cornbread, all to be washed down with a glass of chocolate milk so full it will spill when raised. Our father warned us that eating too much will only make us hungry sooner, which seems counterintuitive, as well as contradictory, since his plate has twice as much food as ours. All of us, in fact, have exceeded our usual amounts, and for the first fifteen minutes we eat with purpose and aggression, as if we've just concluded rather than are about to begin the fast.

Some members of the church fast often, as much as three or four times a week, but on the Day of Atonement it's required of everyone, save the ill and too young. Until now, Bubba and I have only marginally participated, skipping dinner when the holy day begins and resuming our meals at breakfast. But this time our parents want us to go all the way. Mr. Armstrong recently warned that the hour is later than we thought, fueling even more speculation that 1975 will at last be the year. If it is, my parents said, it would be best for Bubba and me to be fully repentant. To be fully repentant, they explained, one has to fast. To survive a fast, Bubba and I decided, we have to rupture our abdominal walls. I nearly succeed. When I rise from the table I'm so stuffed I can't imagine the need to ever eat again.

But now, twenty hours later, I would offer Jesus to the Sanhedrin for a bowl of lima bean stew.

André's on our parents' bed napping while everyone else is in the living room, having decided to ride out the final hours of the fast together. Our parents are on the sofas while Timmy, Bubba, Tommy, Linda, and I are sprawled out on the carpet, dropped here by the bombs of our hunger. Every once in a while a stomach rumbles and we try to guess whose it is, but the game soon loses its appeal. So do Timmy's descriptions of what he's imagining his saliva to be—a piece of steak, a slice of cheese, a bite of chunky peanut butter and jelly sandwich, fried chicken. When he says he's washing it all down with a mouthful of ice-cold beer, our father tells him to shut up. Now the room is quiet, save the clock on the wall, its rhythmic tick our escort through the hours, minutes, and seconds that remain.

At a quarter past four I break the silence. "I'm dying," I say.

"You're not dying," my father responds.

But how else to explain my stomach cramps, and my difficulty breathing? And what else could cause my head to hurt so much, short of an aneurism? "I'm pretty sure I am."

"Me too," Bubba moans. His eyes are rimmed with tears.

Our mother promises us we'll be fine.

Linda reaches toward Bubba and rubs his back. "Maybe they're too young for this," she says. "I mean, they're only ten."

"They're not too young," Tommy responds. "*I* fasted at their age."

He also cheated. So did Mary. For three hours they begged for food so incessantly that when they suddenly fell quiet our mother suspected them of sneaking something from the kitchen. When they denied it, she returned to the basement to continue the laundry, and Mary and Tommy returned to the toilet paper on their laps. They each had already eaten a quarter of their respective rolls and would have eaten more if Linda hadn't walked by to see them pulling off clumps and stuffing it into their mouths like cotton candy. She told our mother, who hurried into the living room just as their violent retching began. Linda, laughing, reminds Tommy of this now.

Tommy tells her to be quiet.

Our father tells Tommy to be quiet.

Linda sticks out her tongue.

Tommy shakes his fist.

"Daddy!" Linda says, "Tommy's shaking his fist at me!"

"Boy, what did I tell you about shaking your fist at your brothers and sisters?"

"She stuck out her tongue!"

A piercing pain grips my stomach and I clutch it with both hands, ready to collect my organs as they push through my skin. "I am dying," I insist. "Does anybody care?"

"Can I please eat something?" Bubba whines.

Timmy tells him to swallow his spit and pretend it is pizza. "Like this," he says. "*Mmmm. Pepperoni!*"

"Shut up, boy!" our father snaps. "Everybody! *Shut up!*"

This time the silence lasts nearly five minutes, until I throw up, the clear bile running down my chin and into my cupped hands. Now Linda rubs my back, telling me I'll be okay, as my stomach continues to heave, pushing up air. She takes me to the bathroom to help me clean up. We return with a cool rag on my head. I sit with her on the easy chair, moaning in agony, as is Bubba. He has moved to the couch next to our mother, his face buried in her bosom, which is where his bile lands a few minutes later. No one vomits after that, but Linda sighs on occasion while Timmy, eyes closed and mouth set in a grin, continues his imaginary feast. The clock ticks on, steadily marching us to sunset, which seems to march steadily away. At last, Tommy announces that it's over. The fast is done.

For hours I imagined how this moment would unfold: my mad dash to the kitchen, the bag of potato chips I'd rip open; the uncooked hot dog I'd devour; the slices of an apple and wedges of an orange; the dill pickle; the Twinkie I'd unearth from my hiding place beneath the sink and swallow whole. But I don't move. No one moves. The most we manage are glances toward the kitchen; even our parents turn their heads that way too. I don't know how much longer we remain here—five, ten minutes?—before our mother finally rises to prepare dinner. Soon we're sitting at the table eating a pauper's meal of tomato soup, crackers, and water. It's the most gratifying meal I've ever had. And at this moment I fully understand the meaning of this suffering: our bodies are impermanent; our lives are fragile; the only things truly worth having are the sustenance God provides and the times we share it with our family. I believe this with all my heart. And I manage to continue doing so for four whole weeks, right up until Halloween.

T he lights are off, signaling that pagans are not welcome here. They come anyway. Every few minutes a mass of bodies marches across the lawn and climbs the stairs, fingers already reaching for the bell. We don't answer. Usually the pagans leave. But sometimes the bell is pressed again, or the door is banged impatiently. Then our father rises from the couch, a print Bible in hand he can't read, there only to emphasize his position and to help shield against evil. As soon as he steps onto the porch the visitors surge forward with their bags extended, and our ears fill with their sinful plea.

Our father explains that it's against our religion to celebrate Halloween. A couple of the older kids always laugh, perhaps believing this is a continuation of the gag that had us bathe our house in darkness. The intention is to give the impression that no one is home, but the effect, for some, is to make the premises foreboding, potentially dangerous, and that draws them to us.

At first they're not disappointed: a grave-looking, blind man clutching a Bible could prove to be the highlight of the evening. And this is even before he mentions the fiery pits of hell. When he does, the laughter starts up again. Our father counters it with scripture, something from the book of Colossians about idolatry and Satan. He usually gets no further than two verses in before the children interrupt him. "Trick or *treat!*" they demand, making it clear the gag has gone on long enough and it's time to stop this crazy talk and deliver the Milk Duds and Snickers.

Each time my father goes outside, I creep close to the door so I can get a better view of their costumes. When he returns, I go back to my post by the picture window next to Bubba. We watch a few kids linger on the porch, still unconvinced that this isn't a trick before they slouch downstairs toward equally perplexed parents, and then everyone moves toward another house, a straggler casting a final glance our way. We wait for the next group, and the scenario is repeated. In the morning our house will be covered with raw eggs, our garbage bins overturned. But at least the holiday will be over.

I hate Halloween. I hate all the pagan holidays, but Halloween is especially difficult to endure because I know in my heart it's harmless fun. Does God really intend to sear the skin off my fifth-grade classmates for cutting witches from construction paper and taping them to the walls? Did he actually write Mrs. Montgomery's name in the Book of Punishment for allowing her students to wear their costumes to school on the day before Halloween? Did he not see how unhappy I was watching my classmates prance around like actors on a stage, a dress rehearsal for the biggest night of the year? Or did he only see my sinfulness, how I longed to be that pirate with a puffy white shirt and plastic sword, or that cowboy in the suede vest and boots with twirling spurs, or that football player in shoulder pads and cleats, or that policeman, or that lumberjack, or maybe even that prostitute who tripped into the room in high heels and a skirt so short that we caught flashes of her underwear before she was sent to the principal's office to wait for her mother to take her home.

Despite my prayers for the strength to not covet these costumes, I wanted them all, and if God would punish me for that sin, he would punish me for this one too: yesterday after school, I stood in my basement's bathroom wearing a wig, pumps, and a dress. The dress was purple with small white flowers; the pumps were black with ribbons on the toes. I think the clothes were Mary's, but they could've been Linda's. I was certain the wig was my mother's. She had several of various styles and colors, and the one I selected had long, brunette curls that fell beyond my shoulders, the same one my father had donned once before sitting at the dinner table, causing Tommy to laugh so hard that the orange juice he'd just swallowed sprayed from his nose. I wondered what Paul's response would be when I emerged from behind the door.

This was his idea. He said he and his little sister dressed up in their mother's clothes and wigs for fun all the time. Since I couldn't officially celebrate Halloween, he reasoned, this would be the next best thing. I agreed to give it a try. I drew the line at his suggestion that I wear panties, though; then he withdrew the suggestion and said only a faggot would wear panties, which he swore he wasn't. I swore I wasn't one either.

"What's a faggot?" I asked Timmy later.

"That's a bad word and you shouldn't use it."

"What does it mean?"

"It's what vulgar people call boys who like boys."

"What's wrong with boys liking boys?"

"Not just liking them," he said. "*Liking* them."

"Okay, so what's wrong with boys *liking* boys?"

He asked me if I knew how babies were made. In my mind flashed a diagram I'd seen in an old biology book of the male and female reproductive systems, each one resembling an aerial view of a highway. I knew that the seed drove from the man's highway to the woman's (though exactly how these highways met was not clear), and then the seed and egg merged to form a kind of tadpole before exiting the woman's highway, now as a fully formed baby, into a doctor's waiting hands. I explained this to Timmy.

"Close enough," he said. "The thing is, some males try to have babies *with other males*, which is impossible because to have a baby you need a seed *and* an egg. The correct name for these men is *homosexual*. God says it's a *terrible* thing to be a homosexual, one of the worst sins imaginable." He got his Bible and found a relevant passage. It was in the book of Leviticus, which didn't surprise me. A lot of terrible sins were in the book of Leviticus. "*'If a man lies with a male as with a woman,'*" he read, "*'both of them have committed an abomination; they shall surely be put to death; their blood is upon them.'*" He looked at me and said sadly, "For your sake, I sure hope you're not a homosexual."

I told him I wasn't. And it seemed prudent not to mention wearing our sisters' clothes and shoes and our mother's wig, or how when I walked past Paul he'd lain on the floor to peek under my dress and once even reached to lift it, or how, when it was his turn to wear the dress, he lifted it again. And while it was true that he wasn't wearing panties, it was also true that he wasn't wearing briefs.

"There," Paul had said when we were finished. "Isn't celebrating Halloween fun?"

It was. I'd known it would be. But I imagined I would've enjoyed it equally as a pirate or a cowboy.

"And the really cool thing," Paul continued, "is that you don't have to wait until Halloween to celebrate it. You can celebrate it anytime you feel like it. Want to do it again tomorrow?"

I did, I told him, but later that night, when the guilt of committing this sin kept me from sleeping, I changed my mind. I rolled onto my stomach and silently prayed for God to forgive me for celebrating Halloween, the worst of the pagan holidays. "But at least," I added, "I'm not a homosexual." I promised to repent, but like so many of my prior promises to repent, this one showed immediate signs of breakage. And so now, as my father stands before trick-or-treaters quoting the book of Colossians, I'm less moved by his warnings of idolatry than by the children's crestfallen faces. And in the morning, while Bubba and I wash our house and clean our lawn, I think about our assailants, imagine God punishing them for throwing eggs and dumping our trashcans, but the overwhelming sadness I feel isn't for them, it's for me.

ONE THIRD OF OUR ENTIRE POPU-
LATION will DIE in this famine and disease
epidemic and along with the coming famine
and disease epidemic will come an invasion of billions
of crop-destroying bugs, insects, and locusts. Once we
are weakened by starvation, disease, and the resulting
calamitous depression, the Ten-Nation European Co-
lossus will suddenly STRIKE with hydrogen bombs
that shall DESTROY OUR CITIES and our centers
of industrial and military production! Simultaneously,
at the very Presence, or Coming, of Christ and all the
holy angels, the seven last plagues of GOD's Terrible
Day of WRATH shall be poured out on the remnants of
the Fascist-Catholic Europe. They will be covered with
BOILS from head to foot. The sea, the lakes, and the
river will become as human blood—all drinking water
will be polluted. This "Beast" power shall have shed the
blood of innocent Christian martyrs—now God will give
them blood to drink!

1975 in Prophecy. I've been rereading it after receiving the
November newsletter, which was particularly ominous; I'm
convinced more than ever that Christ is coming and God
called Mr. Armstrong to warn us in advance. I am tempted

to do a little warning of my own with another sermon, a large one this time, with Paul and some of the neighborhood kids in attendance, but I decide instead to casually mention, at every opportunity, what the next year has in store.

My efforts weren't appreciated. After a few weeks when I'd go outside to join a snowball fight, suddenly someone would be late for piano practice and have to leave. Other kids, not bothering with pretense, simply walked away. Even Paul began remembering neglected chores, vaguely described, that more often than not kept him indoors. It doesn't matter. Any day now my family will be gone, whisked away in a cloud of mist to the Place of Safety.

But the destination isn't the Sahara Desert, as I once believed. Actually, there won't be a cloud of mist either. I've come to understand that as soon as we receive a sign that the Great Tribulation has started, the Co-Workers are to sell all our worldly possessions, withdraw our money from banks, and send everything to Mr. Armstrong for the purchase of a fleet of jumbo jets. We'll load the jets with the provisions that currently cram our basements, garages, and storage sheds, like the canned goods and comic books my family has stockpiled for years. Our destination is to the country of Jordan, to its ancient city of Petra.

Mr. Armstrong visited the site with his wife in 1956, though he mentally visited it long before in this passage from the book of Revelation: "And the woman was given two wings of a great eagle, that she might fly into the wilderness, into her place, where she is nourished for a time, times and half a time from the face of the serpent." The "time, times and half a time" are the three and a half years the Great Tribulation will last. The "woman" is the Worldwide

Church of God. The "great eagle" is a jumbo jet. The "wilderness" is Petra.

We have an old copy of a *Plain Truth* magazine with a photo of Petra on the cover. The image is of one of the rock-hewn facades, at once majestic and foreboding, with the now deceased Mrs. Armstrong standing at its entrance, half-concealed in the shadows. Inside the magazine are additional photos of tombs and caves, of temples once vaulting toward the sky now a tourist's site of ruins, of a vast horizon of rubble and sand. There's an article too, written by the apostle's wife herself, and she describes sleeping in one of the caves and being hungry, cold, and exhausted from the trek, concluding that Petra "was no bed of roses but a place to really rough it."

Sometimes I have trouble reconciling fleeing the Great Tribulation with arriving in Petra only to sleep in the cracks and crevices of stone. But we will, because our ancestors did, the two million Israelites who camped at Petra after their exodus from Egypt en route to the Promised Land. Mr. Armstrong told us that he's already spoken with Jordan's King Hussein about our plans. The king gave his consent, Mr. Armstrong added, but only after learning we're modern-day Israelites and therefore have a right to the land.

So everything is ready on our end, and we've been assured that God has taken care of his. To prevent women from having childbirth during our departure, for instance, and later as we wait for Christ, God will seal their wombs. If we run out of canned goods and fresh water, God will send us more. If we fall ill, God will heal us, though he'll make sure that some Co-Workers are doctors and nurses (these will be okay) because he'll be very busy.

We won't. Not without television or radio, and with only a limited supply of comic books, though I imagine some of our time waiting for the famine, diseases, and wars to run their course will be spent in training, learning all we need to know about being gods. I've outgrown my belief that being a god means being a superhero. I won't get a lightning bolt. I won't get a shield. I probably won't even be able to see through walls. But I will sit in judgment of my peers, determining the fate of every boy and girl I've ever known. This, I've decided, is enough of a superhero for me.

And yet despite how thoroughly our ministers describe the plan, I still don't think it makes complete sense. I just can't understand how *all* the Co-Workers will fit on those planes or why the unconverted will simply let us board them while they remain behind to suffer. And while God will provide the food and water we need, will he also provide beds and clothes? Or maybe, as gods, we won't sleep, but rather we'll patrol the earth nonstop for a thousand years. And maybe our clothes will always be clean. Assuming we wear clothes. Assuming we have bodies. Perhaps, instead of vanishing into a cloud of mist, it is a cloud of mist we'll become.

I ask my parents many of these questions, and they answer them as well as they can, but if I press too hard for logic, they remind me that often the most important part of knowing is simply believing, and I say that believing isn't always knowing, and they ask me, if I'm so smart, would I rather stay behind when it's time to board the planes. I think of living in those dark caves and of sleeping on cold beds of stone, and then I imagine floating downstream in the lake of fire to the waiting hands of Satan. These are my two choices. Sometimes, though, I wonder if there's a third; I can live my life like a normal boy, and the world will simply go on. But who can risk counting on such a thing? I choose to be a believer. I'll be on one of those planes.

January 1975. We spend it waiting for a sign, any sign, of the Great Tribulation. But nothing happens, not even the sighting of a single cloud of locusts. Nothing happens next month either. By March, the restlessness in our congregation, and likely in all the others too, is palpable, and Mr. Armstrong tries to quell it by sending a newsletter that says,

> We are definitely in the END TIME. Conditions are already worse in the world than ever before. We are rapidly moving into the GREAT TRIBULATION of Matthew 24:21–22, when, UNLESS God supernaturally intervenes to STOP IT (cut it short), NO FLESH WOULD BE SAVED ALIVE ON THIS EARTH!
>
> Some years ago I saw factors indicating the possibility that our work might be completed by early 1972, and immediately followed by the Great Tribulation. I NEVER SET A DEFINITE DATE. I NEVER SAID IT WOULD DEFINITELY HAPPEN—but cautioned there were indications of the possibility. Yet some misunderstood and took it as a definite prophecy for a definite date. We need to be careful lest we fall into the fate of the man who said, "My lord delayeth his coming."
>
> The Apostle Paul thought the end of this age and the coming of Christ would occur in his time, 1900 years ago. The apostles all thought it would happen in their day—1900 years ago. But let us beware lest we slack off in OUR PART in backing GOD'S WORK.

Jesus Christ Himself said—and LISTEN CARE-
FULLY to this!—"WATCH therefore: for ye know not
what hour your Lord doth come . . . in such an hour as ye
think not the Son of man cometh. Who then is a faithful
and wise servant [Co-Worker in HIS WORK], whom
his lord hath made ruler over his household, to give them
meat in due season? Blessed is that servant, whom his
lord when he cometh shall find so doing [doing his part in
God's WORK]. Verily I say unto you, That he shall make
him ruler over all his goods. But and if that evil servant
shall say in his heart, My lord delayeth his coming [and
some of you Co-Workers may have thought that]. . . . The
lord of that servant shall come in a day when he looketh
not for him, and in an hour that he is not aware of, And
shall cut him asunder." (Matt. 24:42–51).

Co-Workers, I personally must speed up my activities more and more and drive on harder and harder! We
don't know the exact day that shall FINISH this great
Work—but these world events SHOUT to us that we
are very near the end—that time is growing SHORTER
AND SHORTER.

The only sign Jesus gave by which we may know when
the end of this world is upon us, besides general world
troubles, is that "this gospel of the kingdom" IS now going into all the world for a witness (Matt. 24:14).

In the April newsletter, the Lord's delay is explained. It's
highly probable, Mr. Armstrong says, that the Tribulation
won't occur until he can spread the gospel throughout South
Asia, which God has only recently opened up to him. This
could take a while, he adds, maybe years.

Many Co-Workers don't believe him. Instead, they believe his original prophecy that the Tribulation will start no later than 1975. And they pinpoint the time to the Feast of Tabernacles, our eight-day-long holy observance every fall that represents the prophesized fulfillment of God's Kingdom on Earth. Its conclusion, called the Last Great Day, is symbolic of when the dead will rise to be offered a final chance at salvation, and this year it will fall on the twenty-seventh of September, which Timmy circles in red on his calendar, as countless other Co-Workers, no doubt, circle on theirs.

The closer we get to this date, the more we hear of these kinds of stories: Co-Workers aren't enrolling their children in school; they are quitting their jobs; they are withholding their mortgage payments and spending the money in Atlantic City and Vegas; they are accruing massive debt on luxury cars, jewelry, and dream vacations in Barcelona and the Cayman Islands; they are liquidating assets in preparation to buy the planes. My parents do none of these things. They carry on as usual while awaiting updates from Mr. Armstrong, as if spreading the gospel to South Asia is all that matters to them now. And yet, when the Feast of Tabernacles is finally upon us, they don't speak of South Asia. They speak of Petra, the rock we will soon enter to hide in the dust from the terror of the Lord.

PART II

T his Wisconsin Dells resort is the same one we stayed at the year before, and the year before that. There are fifty-eight Feast of Tabernacles sites around the world, but this is the only one we can afford. Once even this place was beyond our means, so our parents rented a room at a motel not far from our house. Other than being cramped and smelling of cigarettes and body odor, it worked just as well. All that really matters to God is that we be homeless for eight days, a condensed reenactment of what it means to be Israelites forced to take temporary shelter after their exodus from Egypt. As far as I know, we've never had to apply for financial assistance from our congregation in order to keep the feast, as some Co-Workers do. And some Co-Workers just swap homes. Others go to exotic places like Paris and London, and even to Australia. It all comes down to a family's income. We are commanded to save 10 percent of our gross earnings for this purpose, and by the end of the feast it all has to be spent.

We don't have a lot of time to spend it. Twice a day we go to church, held on three hundred acres of land where a few years earlier Mr. Armstrong built a gathering hall. The structure is as nondescript as an airline hanger, and probably larger, capable of holding up to fifteen thousand worshipers. There appear to be that many in attendance, if not on the second day of the feast, when Garner Ted Armstrong flies in to deliver the sermon, then surely on the fourth day, when Mr. Armstrong himself is here. The Feast of Tabernacles is the only time most of us ever get to see him or his son in person, and we appreciate that they always make an effort to visit as many of the American feast sites they can reach in an eight-day span. When we heard there would be twelve American sites, the most ever, I felt pride in knowing that our tithes had helped buy their planes. Still, despite the convenience of their travel, I can't help but wonder how much longer Mr. Armstrong can keep up this kind of a schedule. It's even less clear how he will have the stamina to get the word throughout South Asia. He recently turned eighty-three years old, and as he moves down the aisle to the stage, there's no denying the deliberateness of his gait, his difficulty climbing the stairs to the stage. He gives his sermon while seated in a chair. Several times he loses his train of thought.

Every day after church, with only a few hours left before dark, Bubba and I quickly change out of our dress clothes into T-shirts, jeans, and sneakers and wander the grounds of our resort. We have miles of winding trails to explore, according to the brochure, though we share them with the occupants of several dozen log cabins. Our cabin looks identical to theirs, with its long, sloping roof, stone-faced chimney, and a wraparound porch where, early on the morning of the final day of the feast—the Last Great Day—I stand watching the sky, terrified of seeing it parted by two mighty hands and snatched open like a curtain. But it remains closed. The sun rises as usual, and it's still there when we return from church. An hour before the sun descends on its own accord, our father announces he has a little money left.

We children can spend it in town, he says, before we head home in the morning.

A short while later, Bubba, Linda, and I are in the heart of the tourist strip with Tommy, Timmy, and three of their friends. I recognize one of them from our congregation in Chicago, but they met the other two boys here, which surprises me because they're white. Even though our white brethren are polite during casual encounters, the races aren't supposed to have much social interaction, which should be easy to accomplish, since, by my guess, only a few dozen minorities are here. I noticed how sometimes at church services, as we moved down the aisles, the white brethren averted their gaze, hoping, it seemed, that we wouldn't take the empty seats near them. But it could have been my parents who caused this reaction, because once a black family responded that way to us too. Blindness, I'm learning, causes people as much discomfort as race.

We buy ice cream from a crowded café and eat it while strolling along the pedestrian mall in a throng of tourists, peering into the windows of shops vying for the last of our tithes. Tommy stops when we reach a dilapidated mansion with missing roof shingles and dangling shutters. There are no stairs to the door; to reach it you have to jump onto the porch, which slopes like a funhouse floor and rests on crumbling cinderblocks. To the left of the porch an elderly man sits at a stand smoking a bent-handle pipe. "Only five dollars," he calls to us. "Five dollars to enter the Haunted House."

Linda refuses. She warns Bubba and me not to go either. But Bubba wants to because I do, and I want to because I know there is nothing inside this house, indeed, nothing inside this world, that can scare me more than what I imagined this day would bring. So as Linda moves toward a bench to finish her chocolate pecan, Bubba and I move toward the ticket agent with the other boys. After paying the admission fee, we all mount the porch. Tommy reaches for the doorknob, advising us to stick together. We nod and follow him in.

The foyer is small, barely enough room for us to crowd around a woman in a rocking chair. She wears half bifocals low on her nose, a curly gray wig, and a white shawl that covers her upper body. For the longest time she ignores us, her attention focused on the two knitting needles she holds and the scarf they are creating. Finally, she peers above her glasses. "Seven of you have come," she says. "But not all of you shall leave." She lowers her gaze back to the scarf and resumes poking the yarn with her needles. One of the white kids makes a joke, something about five dollars not going very far these days, and as soon as we laugh we are silenced by a door creeping open to the woman's left. The woman points inside. No one moves. She orders us to enter. The boy who made the joke turns and runs back outside. "Stick together," Tommy says once more. Then we step into the darkness.

The hall is narrow; you can touch each wall without fully extending your arms. We move forward, keeping one hand on the shoulder of the person in front of us, per Tommy's instructions. It's easy going at first, other than not being able to see, and as we inch along, all we have to contend with are high-pitched pleas for help and cries of the torture coming from above our heads. We reach a flight of stairs and take them to the second floor, where we are greeted by more pleas and cries. By now the older kids have composed themselves enough to respond by joking, "Next time study your Bible more!" and "That's what you get for not being a Chosen

One!" It helps too that our eyes have adjusted a little to the darkness. I can see the speakers on the ceilings, emitting the recorded despair. We continue along, a little quicker now, a little bolder in our retorts, until we reach a dead end.

We retrace our steps, come upon a hall that has several options, and debate which one to take. The matter is decided when a wall to our left retracts like a garage door and a flash of light reveals a man with an ax. We flee in all directions, some of us stumbling up stairs, others tripping down, and others—Bubba and me—back to the hall that had led us there, and into the lobby. The woman in the chair says something to us but we don't stop to listen. We do listen to Linda. "I *told* you," she says when we join her and the white kid on the bench. "Now you're going to have a bad dream."

I'm already having bad dreams, I think. So what does it matter if I have one more?

The stones are marshmallow soft and the air smells of spring. Bats are as hospitable as butterflies, landing on my shoulders if I remain still, and the snakes and mice that move over my feet are neither frightened nor frightening. The walls are lined with shelves of food—Twinkies, hot dogs, Neapolitan-flavored cupcakes there for the taking, and not a vegetable in sight. I walk around this place in wonder at the Lord's glory, grateful for the blessings he has bestowed on my family, on all of us Chosen Ones, but mostly I'm relieved I never doubted his word, not really. Deep in my heart, I always believed.

My parents can see. My mother's eyes are brown like mine, though sometimes they are green or blue, and once they are violet like the one I found in her drawer. I like staring into them all. And she likes cupping my cheeks and telling me I am handsome, as she always imagined, and my father tells her that along with eyes, the Lord should have given her good vision.

I have a beautiful bride. It's my sister Mary, of course. She holds my hand when the screams of the unconverted assault our cave, hurled through the entrance where three-headed dogs stand guard. When I hear Paul's voice rise above the others, I touch my face, stroking the smoothness where my scar once was. Mary says we should leave. She leads me into the depths of Petra so that Paul's voice is replaced first by a cascade of water, then by a strum of harps, then by the Jackson 5 singing "I'll Be There," and finally by God reading from the Book of Judgment that I'm not a true believer, listing all my doubts and the times I cried myself to sleep wishing I hadn't been chosen. And then, as the dream always ends, he grabs my arm and tosses me into the sinful masses where I belong, where, he says, I've always wanted to be. Sometimes, when I wake, I can still feel his hand. I feel it now. I reach to touch it. My mother responds.

"I've called you four times," she says. "Now hurry or you'll be late for school."

I roll over to face her. She's standing next to my bed wearing her yellow and white housedress. She's also wearing her dark glasses, hopelessly blind again, and my heart sinks at this reality. I don't want to let go of her, but she eases her fingers from mine and starts to leave.

"I had the bad dream again," I say.

She comes back. "Oh, baby. I'm sorry."

"Why do I keep having it?"

"God's speaking to you," she says, as she has each time before. "He wants you to believe."

"I *do* believe," I say. And I do. Or at least I believe more than the Co-Workers who quit the church eight months ago after the Feast of Tabernacles, or more than the Co-Workers who showed a little more patience by waiting to quit at the year's end. And I might even believe more than Timmy. As soon as we returned from the feast he started skipping church, claiming to be sick. Maybe once or twice he was. But stomach bugs wouldn't be preventing him from reading his Bible, which I know remains untouched on his dresser, because the speck of Kleenex I put on its cover three months ago is still there. He stopped quoting scripture too. He even stopped speaking like an apostle. I try to get him to do it sometimes, greeting him with "How goeth thee?" only to receive a "Hey, man" or "What's up, little bro'?" in response. And the other night I jokingly said, "Strong spirits doeth gladden the heart" when I caught him on the porch with a beer he pilfered from our father, as if a seventeen-year-old drinking a whole can of Schlitz was no big deal. I come close to telling my mother about that beer now, but I don't stop her as she moves toward the door.

After school Bubba and I go to Paul's. Right before we knock on the back door, he opens it, whispers for us to be quiet, and waves us in. We follow him to the unfinished area of the basement used for storage. Beneath the low-hanging fluorescent lights are a few dozen cardboard boxes, discarded toys, a dust-covered rowing machine, and Milo's old bedding from when he was a puppy. I can see Milo in the backyard pacing by the window, his movements restricted by the massive chain attaching him to his doghouse. Directly beneath the window is a closet Paul's father made from two-by-fours and knotty pine. Paul opens its door and unclips a wool skirt from a hanger. He hands it to Bubba. Bubba holds it away from his body with the tips of two fingers like a soiled diaper. Then Paul hands me a skirt and takes one out for himself. He and I begin to undress. I stop at my briefs. Paul doesn't stop at his. Nude, except for an orange T-shirt and white Adidas, he looks at Bubba and says, "Come on. It's fun."

Bubba looks at me.

"Well," I say, "it is."

Bubba removes his pants. The skirt that replaces them is orange and clashes with his red and blue Spider-Man

T-shirt. Paul's skirt is golden brown like sugar. Mine is black and white and made of tweed. It fans from my body when I twirl.

"That's cool," Paul says. "Do it some more."

I do it some more.

"Very cool." Paul steps backward to a corner. "Watch this," he boasts. "I'm going to do a cartwheel." He's good at doing cartwheels, or handstands, or any other form of gymnastics that results in him being upside down, his inverted skirt draped around his torso, his private public. Sometimes his private is stiff. Lately, mine has been getting stiff too, like when I'm in class and Mrs. Morris leans against her desk with as much of her thighs showing as I'm showing now, though it is as likely to became stiff when I open my math book or see a bird fly by the window or scratch my arm. I don't know what to make of this stiffness. But I know that when it arrives I would be more comfortable wearing a skirt without briefs than blue jeans with briefs. Maybe Paul is onto something.

Bubba doesn't seem to like playing Halloween. I didn't think he would, but Paul suggested I bring him. Now he stands with his arms folded across his chest, scowling and silent. There is a slight possibility that he's simply deep in thought, maybe debating between a twirl and a cartwheel. And there isn't necessarily anything to read into his mood; he's been cranky for the last eight months, since the stutter he'd developed a few years earlier turned severe. The speech therapist who examined him couldn't say what suddenly worsened his condition, but emotional trauma was mentioned as a possibility. That made me think of the haunted house, how maybe it was the straw that broke the camel's back.

"This . . . this . . . this . . ." he says, "this . . . is . . . is . . . is . . . *dumb.*"

Paul recommends a cartwheel.

"N . . . n . . . n . . . no."

"Okay. Then just twirl. Show him, Jerry."

I twirl.

"Try that," Paul says.

Bubba shakes his head.

"Well then, how about this." Paul does a jumping jack that merges into a deep knee bend.

Bubba's scowl deepens. "I'm . . . I'm . . . I'm . . ." He abandons the rest of the sentence and changes back into his clothes. After he's gone, Paul observes that playing Halloween isn't for everyone.

It isn't for me either. I've already decided this will be my last game. After the new year started, when I was certain the 1975 prophecy wasn't going to be fulfilled and we had no immediate plans to leave for Petra, I started inviting Paul to play Halloween and used the occasions to distance myself from our church, explaining that I no longer believed in its teachings. It was a harmless lie, I reasoned, but a necessary one for the process of remaking myself. Pretty much all the boys I once knew in the neighborhood had moved, and the ones who replaced them had no knowledge of my religion. I hoped Paul would spread the word that I was normal, or at least not spread the word that I wasn't. And in this way I would slowly integrate myself into the sinful masses, where I belong, where I've always wanted to be.

I 'm reading a comic book on the couch when my father comes home from work so wet from a summer storm that his white dress shirt has turned transparent, revealing his T-shirt beneath, on which is a picture of a naked man and woman. At first I think the couple is wrestling, with the man having pinned his smaller opponent to the floor, but then I close my comic book and move closer to get a better look. No, I conclude, this is something else. I also conclude that my father has mistakenly worn Tommy's T-shirt and that, if this mistake is made known, he will explode.

The last time he exploded was three months ago, on a late afternoon in March. There was precipitation that day as well: large droplets of freezing rain that pelted us as we walked along Seventy-ninth Street, arguing about my new shoes. The shoes were in the box I carried under the arm opposite the one my father held, and at issue was that they weren't the current fashion. They were flats like my father's, like everyone's father's, I supposed—the footwear of old men and of nerds. I was a nerd, it's true, but the process of remaking myself had expanded my sense of what I could become. I could become cool, it had occurred to me. But for that to happen I needed platform shoes. My older siblings wore them, so did most of my friends, so did Don Cornelius and the *Soul Train* dancers. "When you're a dancer on *Soul Train*," my father responded to this last point, "I'll buy you platform shoes. Better yet, I'll buy you *stilts*." He laughed, and I regret that I didn't simply laugh with him. Instead, I led him off the edge of the curb, where his feet plunged into the four inches of slush that, at the last moment, I'd cleared with a short leap. My father shoved me aside, telling me to get away from him, although later, when we were home, he called me back. I found him in his bedroom, removing his belt. He skipped the scripture reading and ordered me to lower my pants and bend over. The welts he left on my backside lasted two weeks. But despite the heavy price I paid, I haven't forgiven myself for what I did. I never will.

But my father forgave me. He forgives all of us for our transgressions, the many violations of his and our mother's trust that provide a counterbalance to our assistance; like the vegetables we've thrown behind the refrigerator, the lights we've kept on after lights-out time, the televisions we've put on mute instead of turning off, the cookies we've snuck from the pantry, the times we've remained silent as our father stood on the porch calling our names when curfew had passed—transgressions we might have always gotten away with if lights and televisions didn't hum, if vegetables didn't rot, if neighbors didn't snitch, if cookies ate themselves. But sometimes we're so guilt ridden that we voluntarily confess our crimes. And sometimes, feeling mischievous, as I am now, we throw each other under the bus.

"Who's here?" my father asks.

"It's me," I say.

"Hi, Jerry," he responds. "Really coming down out there." He sets his briefcase on the floor before folding his cane and hanging it in the closet. "I'm soaked."

"Right down to your T-shirt," I note.

"And to my socks." He kneels and begins unlacing his shoes. "As soon as I left work it started and it hasn't stopped since."

The Lighthouse for the Blind is an hour and a half away by public transportation—a trip that requires two subway trains, a bus, and a three-block walk. During the course of his commute home, he must have encountered hundreds of people. What did they think upon seeing him? I wonder. That he was a hippie? A swinger? A madman? An undercover cop? Did they scamper to get away from him, as people often do when a blind person approaches, or did they, like me, move closer to get a better look?

"How was the trip?" I ask.

"Long," he says. His shoes are off now. He turns and walks through the living room.

I follow him, stifling a giggle. "Anything . . . you know . . . um . . . *bizarre* happen along the way?"

The question must strike him as odd, if not because it is, then because of my halting delivery. He pauses and faces me. We're in the hall, his bedroom just to his left. I can hear my mother's voice through the opened door as she talks on the phone. "No," he says, "nothing *bizarre* happened. Why do you ask?"

"Well . . . your T-shirt's sort of . . . visible."

"And?"

"There's a picture on it."

"A picture? A picture of what?"

"Of a man," I say. "And a woman."

"Who are they?"

"I don't know."

"What are they doing?"

I hesitate, trying to think of the most delicate way to break the news. My father loses his patience.

"*What are they doing?*" he demands.

I say, "Making love." I don't recall having ever spoken these words before, but in this era of Motown and rhythm and blues I have surely sung them. It's such a beautiful phrase, I believe, one associated with tenderness and caring, and this makes the contrast between it and my father's reaction all the more stark. He swears and begins removing his dress shirt, fumbling with the buttons before giving up midway and yanking the remaining ones free. When the shirt is off and balled at his feet, he snatches the T-shirt over his head so violently it tears, which sets in motion a tearing frenzy. By the time he goes into his bedroom, the culprit is on the floor in quarters. I pick them up and throw them away, smiling at the thought of Tommy's fate, and already knowing that, despite my father's rage, he will forgive this too.

I go back to the couch. As I reach for my comic book, I imagine my father on its cover—stance wide and hands on hips as he rides the bus in his pornographic T-shirt, and his eyes, functioning now, scan the faces of the commuters, taking in their wonder that he, Captain Love, the world's greatest superhero, is actually here.

Tommy's driving. My father is to his right. My mother is in the second row between Linda and me, while Bubba and André ride behind us, facing the speeding traffic that will crush me if my dangerous game goes awry. My suit jacket is bunched up to the right of my lap, concealing the handle of the door I'm holding to keep it from swinging wide open. It's easy to keep the door steady while the car goes straight or makes right turns. The difficulty is during left turns, when centripetal force comes into play and threatens to pull me to the street.

Timmy isn't with us. He's "sick" again, his fourth time out of the last six church services. The two times he attended he sat in the rear of the auditorium with a few other teenagers who wore similar disaffected expressions. Once, when I looked over my shoulder, he was gone. He didn't return until near the sermon's end, as we were about to sing the closing hymn. Later, when I asked him where he was, he said he'd felt nauseated and had gone outside for some air.

Something causes Bubba and André to giggle. Linda turns to see what it is, but I can't let myself be distracted. I have to concentrate, like Tommy. He sits as fixed as a statue, squeezing the steering wheel as I squeeze the door handle, commanding silence lest he lose focus and hit a tree. As an inexperienced driver, his hitting a tree is a real possibility, though spontaneous laughter would less likely be the cause than mechanical failure. We're in a 1964 Ford Fairlane, equal parts paint and rust, with a low-hanging muffler that clanks against bumpy roads and, on inclines, coughs gray smoke. At times the engine shakes so violently that the windows rattle, and the vinyl seats have deep rips, the foam inside visible like tissue in a wound. My parents saved this car from the junkyard four years ago when Mary got her license. The plan was for her and, later, Tommy to drive us to and from church so we wouldn't have to rely on Mr. Martin or the St. Claires, but because the car itself is so unreliable, we try to use it only as a last option, as it is today. The St. Claires are under the weather, and Mr. Martin is gone.

I miss Mr. Martin. He was so kind to my family, so quick to give my parents assistance whenever they asked for it, always ready with a piece of butterscotch candy at the exact moment I needed one. The whole congregation loved and respected him. After he missed two consecutive services and talk of cancer spread, prayer groups were formed on his behalf, and if it had been okay for him to see an oncologist, a medical fund surely would've been started. In the third week of his absence, when the minister prefaced his sermon by saying, "I begin this morning with bad news," I feared we were about to learn of his death. It was worse. "In accordance with the doctrine of our church," the minister continued, "it is my duty to inform you that Mr. Martin has been disfellowshiped." Over the gasps and murmurs, the minister instructed us to have no communication with Mr. Martin. If he phoned us, we weren't to speak to him. If we saw him in public, we were to ignore him. We were advised to not even say his name.

Yes, this is worse than death, because death doesn't have to be final. When Jesus returns at the millennium, everyone who walked the face of the earth will be given a second chance at life, unless they voluntarily quit God's true church, or, like Mr. Martin, received a visit from the deacons, their fingers parting the pages of Bibles that described some unpardonable sin. Prior to Mr. Martin, my parents said, this had happened only once in our congregation, and it was long before I was born, back when the penalty for interracial unions was much more severe. A parishioner in our congregation had appeared at a church picnic holding hands with a white woman and introduced her as his new bride. Even before the hot dogs were served, the newlyweds were told to leave the grounds. The deacons paid them a visit the next day. The couple wasn't seen again.

I saw Mr. Martin. It was a month after his disfellowship. I was at the grocery store with my mother, about to read her the ingredients of a can of chili when he entered our aisle. I told my mother and asked what we should do. Ignore him, she said. I drew the can closer to my face and began to read, but I couldn't concentrate enough to get beyond *modified cornstarch*, so I repeated this until Mr. Martin stopped at our side. He cleared his throat. My mother turned her head. I continued staring at the can. Our response to him was heartless, it seemed, because Mr. Martin had been our friend, but what was friendship when the penalty of communicating with the disfellowshiped was to become disfellowshiped? Mr. Martin knew this penalty too, and I felt my unease of his presence turning to resentment until, against my better judgment, I looked at him. But I was mistaken; it wasn't him. I suddenly wished it were. I wanted to tell him good luck and to thank him for all he'd done for my parents, and even though I wouldn't have been able to say these things, I hoped that, by accepting a piece of his butterscotch candy, he would've understood that I had.

We heard he moved. Some accounts had him in California. Other accounts had him in Florida. All accounts had him speaking out against the church, calling Mr. Armstrong a liar and fraud. We never learned what drove Mr. Martin to this heresy; after the announcement of his disfellowship, the minister had only reminded us that to publicly criticize the church or Mr. Armstrong was to raise a voice against God. My father repeated this phrase later that evening, and then he extended it by saying to criticize him, as head of the household, was to raise a voice against God too. Then Tommy said, "Ditto for criticizing the firstborn son," which would have been funny if he'd been joking, as it would have been funny if he were joking about hitting a tree.

He doesn't hit a tree. He hits the curb in front of our house at the very instant I relax my grip on the door, causing it to snatch free and swing wide open. When he whirls around to face me, his expression of shock quickly gives way to a grin, and I know he's remembering how I got him in trouble about the pornographic T-shirt. "Daddy!" he yells, "Jerry never closed his door! He rode all the way home with his door open! He could have fallen onto the street! He could have been *killed!*"

I picture myself prone on the expressway, a pool of blood beneath my crushed skull. Then I picture myself prone on my father's bed with my pants around my ankles, his belt splitting my skin. But either I'm getting too old to be spanked or my father is getting too old to spank me, because all he does is send me to my room for the rest of the day, no food, no television, no one to keep me company, disfellowshiped, like Mr. Martin, only to a lesser degree.

The maple has lost most of its leaves. A strong wind attacks the survivors. I fix my attention on one near the top of the tree and watch its futile struggle while the counselor urges me to describe my long-term goals. He doesn't know I've spent almost thirteen years believing that at any moment the sky would collapse into a fiery tornado and obliterate much of mankind; long-term goals aren't something I've given a lot of thought to. I don't know where to begin. He's telling me to begin somewhere, though, because he believes I have academic promise. He's not alone. During the three days since the results of a standardized test were publicized, teachers have congratulated me as I walk through the halls, and if it was my first time meeting them, they shook my hand and said, "So *you're* the one." It made me uncomfortable being singled out this way when, for my whole life, all I've wanted was to fit in.

My leaf loses its battle. As it sails out of view I look from the window to my hands and begin counting the ridges of my fingerprints as I used to do in church. The counselor presses me. "Well," he's saying, "when you were younger, was there something you wanted to be more than anything else?"

"Yes."

"And what was that?"

I look up. "A god."

He smiles. "How about something a little less grand?"

"Captain Marvel."

His smile fades as he leans forward, places his elbows on his desk, and rests his chin on his entwined fingers. "Just give me your thoughts on college. And don't tell me you don't have any. Even the kids who are flunking seventh grade have thoughts about college."

I don't want to disappoint this man, to contradict his impression of me as worthy of his time, but I have no thoughts about college, other than vague notions of it spawned by Mary. "My plan," I say, "is to attend Indiana University."

"Okay then," he says, "that's a start. What do you want to study?"

"Music."

"Good, good, good."

"So, basically," I continue, relieved to have this ready-made narrative at hand, waiting only to be presented, "my long-term goal is to be an elementary school music teacher."

"That's fantastic. What instruments do you play?"

I don't play any. Mary plays the piano, bassoon, and clarinet. I tell him these.

"Very impressive," he says. "Only set your sights higher than Indiana U. It's a fine school, but you should be thinking Julliard or Berkeley. Maybe Oberlin. I'll send for some brochures." He takes a maroon fountain pen from his shirt pocket and begins writing on a pad of paper. And then he drops a fiery tornado of his own, obliterating my vague belief that, should I find myself in a future called 1978, it would be as a freshman at South Shore High. That's where Mary and Tommy went, and where Timmy and Linda are now. "I've spoken with the principal of Whitney Young High. He wants you there next year."

"Next year? I'll be in eighth grade next year."

"You scored high enough on the exam to place out of eighth grade." Now he speaks about Whitney Young High, describing it as a competitive magnet school known for attracting the top students in the city, none of whom, to his knowledge, have ever come from here. "You'll be our first," he says. He smiles and adds, "You're the one."

I *am* the one.

"You're the *what*?" my father asks.

"The one," I repeat. "The counselor said so. Some of the teachers too."

It's the morning after I met with the counselor. I barely slept last night thinking about Whitney Young, this academic version of the Kingdom of Heaven we've so far been denied. Things could be perfect for me there. I probably wouldn't be teased for liking school, as I am now, or for reading novels that haven't been assigned, or for speaking like a white boy, as the black boys who've moved to the neighborhood say I do. I bet everyone at Whitney Young speaks the same way, or maybe everyone speaks differently and it doesn't matter anymore than a lion will matter to a lamb in the coming Eden. But the campus is all the way across town on the West Side, near the housing project where I was born, and there's no chance my parents will let me travel that far alone. I've come to their bedroom to confirm this. As I stand at their door waiting for their response, I'm experiencing a strong sense of déjà vu; my mother is sitting in the rocker with a book of scripture on her lap, and my father has one on his stomach as he lies on their bed, the exact positions I found them in six years earlier when I came to ask about going to Paul's for Christmas. The thought enters my mind that the devil is tempting me with this school the way he tempted me with Paul's toys. Some terrible fate awaits me there. And so when my parents surprise me by saying yes, I can go, I've already decided I won't.

Now it's a day later and I'm back in my counselor's office. He's studying my face, waiting for it to relax into a smile before I admit I'm joking. When neither happens, he says, "Are you serious?"

"Yes."

"Why won't your parents let you go?"

I look out the window and speak to the barren maple. "They want me to attend South Shore, like my brothers and sisters."

"That's not a good reason."

"They also said I'm too young to travel that far by myself."

When I look back at the counselor, he's shaking his head but stops and says, "Maybe I should call them."

"That won't help. There's no chance they'll change their mind."

"Do they understand what this opportunity could mean for you?"

"Apparently not," I say sadly.

He shakes his head some more and hasn't stopped by the time I excuse myself and leave.

I hope he doesn't call. The last thing I need is to be caught in a lie. My mother is already disappointed with me for saying I don't want to go, and my father got so upset that I had to promise I'd think about it some more. But there's nothing more to think about. I've made up my mind. This is Satan's plan, it's clear to me, and I put my decision not to attend Whitney Young squarely on his shoulders.

ecember. Timmy's Saturday sicknesses have spilled over into Sundays, so along with church he's missing basketball games. Finally he quits the team outright, as Tommy already has, though Tommy's reasons aren't suspect. When he finished high school last year, he enrolled in a technical college for computer programming. To help pay for his classes he began working Sunday mornings bagging groceries at a local supermarket. So only Bubba and I continue to play basketball for the church, though not well enough to have a positive impact on the games. It would help if we attended practice more regularly, but it's too tempting to sleep in rather than be at the bus stop at 6:30 a.m., especially now that it's winter. Bubba fell to that temptation this morning. I'm out here alone.

The temperature's in the teens. The snow, at least a foot deep, is so difficult to walk through that the man who suddenly appears at my side is almost too out of breath to say he has a gun. He puts me in a headlock and drags me to a nearby alley. When he releases me and begins punching my face, all I can think about is a recent newsletter from Mr. Armstrong warning that The End will be precipitated by a spike in the level of man's violence against man. Perhaps this is the sign we've been waiting for.

The man stops punching me so he can search my pockets. After finding only six dollars and a bus transfer, he yells, "This *all* you got?" I don't know what he was expecting. And I can't imagine how much more he needs, since a pint of wine only costs a dollar, which I know because I've seen men pay that amount at the corner store where I get my candy. There have been more and more of these men lately, and it's gotten to the point where it's nearly impossible to make a Twinkie run without someone leaning into my face asking for spare change. I try not to inhale when they talk, because their breath usually smells of liquor, tobacco, and vomit, like my robber's. "*Give me your shoes!*" he demands. I give him my shoes. "*Give me your coat too!*" I give him my coat. He turns and lumbers through the alley's snowdrifts with my possessions. I return to the bus stop.

God is merciful. Even though I'm crying, the man's blows didn't actually hurt that much, and I don't feel the slightest bit cold, despite not having a coat or shoes. I don't have to wait long for the bus either. And the driver God sends is a compassionate, elderly man who gives me Kleenex to wipe my bloody face and drops me off between stops, right at the field house door. Before I disembark, he shakes his head and mutters, "What's the world coming to?"

"The End?" I offer.

I say it with more conviction when I reach the gym. My coach and teammates have crowded around me, and I explain that Mr. Armstrong warned of things like this. "Remember?" I ask. "The August newsletter? Or was it September's?"

"Let's get you cleaned up," the coach says, "then I'll take you home."

Once home, after giving my parents and siblings an account of what happened, I write Mary. Lately our correspondences have fallen off, probably because there isn't enough going on in either of our lives to put to paper. At least now I have a good story. She responds immediately, saying she's sorry about what happened but relieved I'm okay. She adds something about her classes being interesting and mentions a citation she earned for playing the bassoon. She closes the letter by saying she'll visit in January, which cheers me up until I see the PS: "I have a surprise!" I don't want a surprise. I know it'll be a boyfriend, some dumb heathen she hopes to bring with her to Petra.

Three weeks later, when I walk into the kitchen for breakfast, she's sitting at the table with my father drinking coffee. I don't see her boyfriend enter the room. I don't hear him. Like the robber on that December morning, he simply appears at my side, here to take from me a thing that is mine. "Hi, there!" Mary says, rising to hug me, and in the seconds it takes my gaze to fall from her smile to her swollen belly, the pedestal I placed beneath her long ago is gone.

M y nephew is born in March. His first name is Jamil, which I like, but his middle name is Kwende. It's African, Mary says, common among the Bantu tribes of the sub-Sahara and infused with great meaning, something about strength, pride, and warrior sensibilities, though what it really means is that she, along with a hundred million other people, saw the television series *Roots*.

My mother wasn't one of them. She was worried the series would be upsetting, and we weren't supposed to be upset by slavery because we were taught it was biblically ordained. I didn't share her concern about being upset, mainly because I don't think of myself as a descendant of slaves. I'm first and foremost a Chosen One, a member of the Lost Tribes of Israel, which means I have less in common with Kunta Kinte, in my view, than with Noah, Lamech, Seth, and Methuselah.

I don't even feel a kinship with my cousins. Aside from being pagans, many of them curse, smoke cigarettes and marijuana, and drink heavily. And they make fun of us, especially for not eating soul food, the chitterlings, pork chops, and fried catfish that are staples of every extended-family gathering. Timmy made the mistake once of offering a scriptural defense of our dietary practices, referring to land animals with cloven hooves that chew the cud, and then he spoke of the abomination of fish without fins and scales, though he stopped short of saying it's okay to eat locusts and crickets, perhaps only because we never have. Over our cousins' laughter, he directed them to read Leviticus.

Our cousins intimidate me. Their West Side neighborhood intimidates me, and it has ever since I was old enough to know what a ghetto is and how dangerous it is to be in one. Each time we drive to my relatives' homes through the grimy streets, menacing-looking men on porches stare our way, drunks sleep in gutters or on bus-stop benches, nearly naked women climb in and out of idling cars, half-charred buildings threaten at any moment to complete the demolition begun by rioters a decade before. Pimps, addicts, pushers, gangs—they're all there in abundance, and it horrifies me to know that my family and I once lived among them. But the fact that we moved to a white middle-class community is the greatest source of teasing of all. We're accused of distancing ourselves from our people, of turning our backs on black traditions and culture, the same charges leveled against my parents after they were called to our faith.

When my mother told me this I was six, having just expressed my first curiosities about how she and my father were saved. "Everyone said we were putting on airs," she'd explained.

"What's 'putting on airs'?" I asked.

"Putting on airs," she said, "is when you stop being a pagan."

She was ashamed of having been one. I was ashamed of her too. And of my father. And of Mary, Tommy, and Timmy, since they were born before my parents were called and had received a fair dose of paganism from the Sanctified

Church. They received even stronger doses of it from the local elementary school, where they, and later Linda, sat in classes with the future addicts, dope dealers, prostitutes, and pimps. Luckily, we moved before Bubba and I started kindergarten, although if we hadn't, perhaps visiting the ghetto wouldn't be so frightening, and perhaps it wouldn't be so frightening now that the ghetto is following us to South Shore.

But at least I have experience being teased. So it doesn't bother me too much when the teenagers who moved to our neighborhood laugh about Bubba's and my ignorance of black culture, which, like my cousins, they've reduced to being a matter of foods and vices. Besides, by now I've come to accept the truth that resides at the mockery's core: we're not black, not in any meaningful sense, and I, for one, have no desire to be.

And so when my mother announced she was boycotting *Roots*, I said I was too. The night it aired she and I sat at the kitchen table to play Scrabble. I wasn't sure where Tommy and Timmy were, but Linda, Bubba, and even André, now five, sat in front of the living room console with our father. The volume was high enough that I heard when the show was about to begin. As it did, I excused myself to get another slice of cheese pizza from the box on the coffee table. I entered the living room and snuck a glance at the screen: a man was walking through a dark jungle, a child in his arms. A caption faded into view: "African Inspiration" followed by two others: "Kunta Kinte: Newborn African" and "Ritual of Spiritual Blessing." When the man reached the top of a mound, he removed the baby from his blanket, held him high above his head, and said, "Kunta Kinte. Behold, the only thing greater than yourself." I went back into the kitchen. My mother had already taken eight little squares from the bag and spread them before her, and now she moved her fingers over each one, reading the Braille letters.

I'd forgotten my pizza. I told my mother, and she said, "You can watch it if you want to."

"No thanks," I said. "Not interested." I reached into the bag and pulled out two squares, an L and an H.

"We can play some other time. I don't mind."

I looked into the living room. I could only see Linda and my father sitting on the couch. I turned back at my mother. "Maybe for just a minute or two."

"That's fine," she said. "But I can't watch it. It'd be too much for me."

It was as brutal and heart wrenching as my mother feared. I tried not to let it affect me, and for the most part it didn't. And yet there were moments when I felt the pressure on my wrists as slaves had theirs bound, and the burn on my back when whips bore into their flesh, and the ache in my gut when families, families that looked like mine, were torn apart and sent to distant lands, never to see each other again.

A month after we turn thirteen, our father gives Bubba and me a brochure that explains the penis's role in being fruitful and multiplying. There will be trial runs, the brochure says, some of which we will have no control over, as they will occur while we sleep, and some of which will be self-induced, and these we will have control over, but not much. The brochure stresses that trial runs are normal, which would have been a good thing to know when we turned twelve so I wouldn't have been consumed by this warning of Apostle James: *"But each person is tempted when he is lured and enticed by his own desire. Then desire when it has conceived gives birth to sin, and sin when it is fully grown brings forth death."*

I don't think my sin was fully grown at twelve, but I knew it was getting close when the image of Mary sitting topless before her dresser returned to me in a dream. I woke in a midst of a trial run, and the shame I felt was unspeakable. The next night I read sports articles by flashlight until the early morning hours, hoping to direct my subconscious to a place of right and purity. It worked. The dream didn't repeat itself. For the last year, reading myself to sleep has been my bedtime routine.

But nothing can stop the trial runs, with their random and ill-timed arrivals, each one a reminder that the devil does not rest. He seems to have set his sights on teenaged males; Bubba told me he was having trial runs, I have seen it happen to Paul, and some of my classmates speak of it openly, explaining with vulgar phrases how they make it go away. Thanks to our youth minister, I know the proper word for what they describe is *masturbation*. It was our youth minister, in fact, who cited Apostle James's warning, then offered that boys who waste their seed will experience blurred vision. I didn't understand at the time the relationship between wasting one's seed and blurred vision, but now, having succumbed to the sin once or twice, it makes sense why the words of my sports articles sometimes melt together. I've taken up the habit of blinking rapidly, a kind of exercise for the pupils, and I've decided to exercise my soul by offering the Lord a harsh penance: for a full month I will not read a novel, or Linda's diary.

Neither will be easy. I read a novel a week, sometimes two. I read Linda's diary daily. At first her life was interesting only in that it was hers; no one else's account of cute boys and deceitful girls could have continued to draw me to its pages. Then she met John, a senior whose hobbies were basketball, checkers, and trying to kiss her. He'd succeeded in kissing her only once so far, a stealthy plant on her right cheek during their history class. Encouraged by the experience, he slipped her a note an hour later, asking to go all the way. She told him no, that she was not that kind of girl, and yet, Dear Diary, *Dear God*, she sometimes wanted to say yes! Since that revelation I have lived for each new entry, eager to see if John has succeeded and, more important, if Linda has failed, because premarital sex is a capital sin, punishable by eternal death, a fate, I fear, that now awaits Mary, even though she married the father of her son.

It's concern for Linda's life, I rationalize, and not a willful breaking of my penance, that leads me to her room after only a three-day absence. I lock the door behind me in case she comes home early, though the likelihood of this is nonexistent. She has band practice. It won't finish until 3:00, another hour and fifty-four minutes away, as indicated by the clock on her nightstand, the very nightstand where she keeps her diary.

I don't rush to the prize. There is no need. Besides, I like the feeling of mounting suspense, of letting my anticipation drive me to a near frenzy before breaking my will. This makes it all the more devastating when, after a few seconds of rummaging through the dresser, I open the nightstand drawer and find it empty. I lift her pillows. I look between the box spring and mattress. I check the closet shelves, dig through a pile of books on the floor, and inspect the windowsill behind the curtains. I search the drawers of her chest, working my hand through the tightly packed clothes, until at last, beneath a tangle of socks, I feel something and pull it free. It's her diary, yes, but there's something else too. A dirty magazine.

I've seen one before. A week earlier my classmate Rodney Morgan snuck a *Playboy* to school; I entered the bathroom just as he announced to a dozen of our classmates that he stole it from his father's collection. Despite my impulse to turn and leave, I joined the boys as they moved to Rodney's side, crouched with them after he placed the magazine on the black and white tiles. While we peered over his shoulder, he turned the pages with such delicacy, such reverence, that we might have been biblical scholars, dumbstruck by our discovery of the Dead Sea Scrolls. When the sacred viewing was over, Rodney began tearing out pages and offering them to us for our personal use. I said I didn't want one, until someone scoffed and accused me of being afraid of girls, so I took it. But before I got home I threw it away. To discover the work of the devil was one thing, to own it quite another. I'm also afraid of girls.

Linda's magazine has none. A shirtless male is on its front and back covers, and much less modest men on the pages in between. I can't believe my sister possesses such vulgarity, such filth, such unlikely stories, I notice, as I begin reading one. It's about a lonely housewife who answers her front door one morning to see a deliveryman in need of a signature for a package. She doesn't think it's odd that he has no package, and he doesn't think it's odd that she wears only lingerie. She invites him to wait inside while she searches for a pen. He checks his watch, sees that he is a little ahead of schedule, steps into the foyer, and stares lustfully at her backside as she climbs the stairs. When she returns a moment later, with a pen but without the lingerie, she finds the deliveryman with his pants and briefs around his ankles and making good use of a trial run, just as Linda finds me when she enters her room.

God is not merciful. If he were he wouldn't have canceled her band practice that afternoon. Or, having canceled it, he would have had the lock on her door hold. Instead, he allows my sister to catch me in this disgraceful act, and her shriek so compounds my humiliation that I pray for the death Apostle James promised. God is not merciful in this regard either. Two hours after Linda has run from her room and I to mine, I'm still alive. I give God four more hours to reconsider before I go downstairs for dinner.

Linda continues to hide her diary. I continue to find it. So I know her latest obsession is a bodybuilder named Stan long before he tackles me in my front lawn that spring and threatens to break my legs. "I told your sister I'd make a man out of you," he says, straddling my chest. "But I can see that won't be easy." What he sees is eighty pounds of skin and bones. What I see is excess muscle beneath a tight T-shirt. He asks me if I am homosexual. I might have asked him the same.

Instead, I profess my heterosexuality, of which I'm largely sure, though my lack of romantic encounters with the opposite sex has left room for doubt. I've never kissed a girl. I haven't even so much as held a girl's hand. If this is typical heterosexual behavior for a thirteen-year-old boy, one wouldn't know it from listening to Paul. Lately he's been boasting about fondling a seventeen-year-old named Rachael who recently moved into the house next to his. I would have dismissed his claims as fantasy if other boys hadn't also made them. I tell Stan about her now, inserting myself as the protagonist of their stories. He wants specifics. "Well, her breasts," I say, "feel like marshmallows."

He looks skeptical. Are marshmallows too soft? "Firm marshmallows," I say.

"You bullshitting me?"

I say I'm not.

"If you're *not* bullshitting," he says, "then that's not too bad. But when I was your age, I'd already popped my cherry."

I don't like the sound of that. So I'm relieved when he changes the subject to muscles, even if only to note the absence of mine. He alternately flexes his pecs, causing them to rise and fall, like beating woofers. "Don't you want to be able to do that?" he asks.

"No, thank you."

"Well, like it or not," he says, "you will."

The next morning he takes me to the YMCA. We lift weights, punch bags, run laps, jump rope, and on the way home, share a thermos of milk and raw eggs. I'm so sore the next day I can barely move. The remedy for the soreness, he says, is to work out some more, so we work out some more, and some more the next day. After four weeks of working out he buys me a weight set of my own so I can put in some extra time. The weights are of poor quality, made of plastic filled with cement. The cement begins to crumble after only two months, which is longer than it takes for Linda to dump him and find a new boyfriend, and for me to catch Rachael's eye.

ome rough kids have moved into the apartment buildings at the end of our block. They like to gather at the open trunk of a blue Chevy, where they keep a cooler of beer, listening to music and sharing pot and cigarettes. When I pass by they invite me to join them, but I keep walking, my head down, bracing for the laughter that follows like clockwork five seconds after I decline. When I'm not in the mood for ridicule, I'll take one of the streets parallel to ours, like Yates or Essex Avenue, or, as I am now, I'll just walk through the alley, admiring, as I go, the landscape of some of my neighbors' backyards. Rachael, I see, is in hers.

"Hey, there," she calls as I reach her gate. She's standing near a blooming row of hydrangeas, an unlit cigarette in hand. In my hand is a bag of groceries, including a few frozen items that I need to get inside. I can't be delayed.

"Come here."

But what will it say about me if I decline her invitation on account of thawing potpies?

"Hey, you."

Am I using this as an excuse because I'm homosexual?

"*Hey*, come here."

Am I fated to lie with men and, as Leviticus warns, be put to death?

"Come *here*."

There's also this: I'm pretty certain scripture makes it clear that a man shouldn't fondle a woman unless she's his wife, and, even then, only during the act of procreation.

"Are you deaf?"

I'm getting ahead of myself. She could just intend to say hello, or maybe she wants to know if I have any matches. I'll simply tell her I don't have any and be on my way. I approach her slowly. She, in turn, moves slowly toward her house, pausing to summon me with a finger.

She has matches. Her cigarette's already lit by the time she sits at her picnic table, her back against the faded pine. She wears cutoff blue jeans, her long light-brown legs glistening in the sun, and a yellow T-shirt nearly as tight as Stan's. Her breasts press against the thin material, unimpeded by a bra. "My potpies are going to melt," I tell her, "if I don't get them inside."

Rachael says, "This won't take long."

"They're melting already, actually."

"What's your name?"

I tell her.

"You live on this block, don't you, Jerry?"

I nod, and for some reason I point in the direction of my house, specifically toward my second-floor bedroom window. I imagine being up there now, wishing, as I have so often before, that I were down here with her. I prefer that scenario. Maybe it's better to want than to receive.

"My name is Rachael."

"I know."

"How do you know?"

"Paul told me."

She smiles, revealing teeth and gums in equal measure. "What else did Paul tell you?"

"That was all, basically." The groceries are getting heavy but I don't want to put them down. I move the bag to my other hand.

"You have tone muscles."

"Well, I work out. So."

"It shows."

I think to flex my pecs, but Stan never got the chance to show me how. I shift the bag, lift it a little, curling it like a dumbbell, to make one of my new biceps rise.

"Do you think I'm pretty?" she asks.

She has nice lips, which are full and moist, but her eyes are close together and her face is on the pudgy side. Her nose is big. There is a large pimple on her chin. She isn't very pretty. "You're very pretty," I say.

She rises, places a hand on her hip and pulls her shoulders back like a pinup girl. "Do you like my figure?"

I nod.

"Do you want to touch me?" She takes a drag from her cigarette and exhales a tight stream of smoke into my face. I struggle not to cough. "You can touch me if you want to. Right here." She points at her left breast, her finger an inch from her nipple. "But only *once*," she instructs me, "this time."

I shift the bag again.

"Hurry up," she tells me, smiling. "You don't want those potpies to melt, do you?"

Never mind the potpies. I'll be doing the melting, either for fornicating or, by not fornicating, tipping the scales toward homosexuality. I'm damned if I do and damned if . . .

She takes my free hand and places it on her. I let it remain. I dart another glance toward my house, and then toward the windows of her house overlooking the backyard, and finally toward the sky. The coast is clear, other than God Almighty.

"You like that?"

I nod.

"How's it feel?"

"Actually," I say, "like a marshmallow."

"A *marshmallow?*" she chuckles. "Never heard *that one* before." She covers my hand with hers and moves it in slow circles. After some seconds she releases me to continue the motion on my own. I improvise a little by reversing direction, then she tells me to squeeze her nipple, and I do, gently, feeling it stiffen between my trembling thumb and index finger. I can sense a stiffness of my own coming on, but I don't care. I don't care about anything, because as of this moment I'm a man, and didn't Mr. Armstrong, just this past April, write in the newsletter that when a man has personal needs they should be fulfilled? Then he announced that after being a widower for ten years, he plans to remarry, and we understood that his personal needs must be very great because his bride is forty-seven years his junior. Mr. Armstrong would approve of what I'm doing, I tell myself. This means God probably does too.

I sit the groceries on the ground and place my free hand on Rachael's other breast. She allows me to grope her like this for several minutes, and through it all she keeps at her cigarette, long drag after long drag, followed by streams of smoke, released into my face.

From a certain angle, it occurs to me later, it must have looked as if God had rendered his judgment on my manhood, setting me aflame.

S preading the gospel throughout South Asia must be going well, because it hasn't been mentioned in the newsletters for two years. But suddenly, in January 1978, Mr. Armstrong announces that the preliminary stages of the Great Tribulation have at last begun. The time has come for more fasting and prayer, he says, and, if we can spare it, more tithes. We can spare it. Our father has gotten a raise. It's not much, but it's enough to offer a little more support of the Great Commission and to put some aside to convert the basement storage space into a bedroom. By October, the Tribulation hasn't noticeably progressed, but the bedroom is done.

Tommy and Timmy share it. Tommy keeps his half neat and notices anything moved from its proper place, such as his album collection, which I move often because some of them have seminude women on the covers. Timmy, on the other hand, is a slob and hoarder. There's always some new thing beneath his bed waiting to be inspected: a pair of brass knuckles, bamboo wind chimes, a telescope with a high-powered lens, a golf putter. And every now and then there's a bottle of liquor that years of tasting my father's beer have made me disposed to sampling. I put the bottle to my lips and tilt it just enough to let the contents hit my tongue,

though sometimes my tongue is out of position and the con-
tent that slips by has to be swallowed. But I've never been
drunk, as far as I can tell.

Timmy has. It's not unusual to find him stumbling around
the house, often with the inebriant still in hand. If my parents are present, he'll wink and hold a finger to his grinning
lips. This isn't the Timmy I grew up with. The Timmy I
grew up with interrupted our father's hillbilly singing with
a proverb about drunkards coming to poverty. That Timmy
planned to study theology at Ambassador College instead of
mathematics at the Illinois Institute of Technology, where
he attends now on a full scholarship, completing his sophomore year. That Timmy took me on as his pupil. Maybe it's
my nostalgia for the old Timmy that makes me willing to be
his pupil again, even if I suspect, from the moment he gives
me my first reading assignment, that these lessons will lead
to my ruin.

When I finish the book I bring it to his room. He's re-
laxing on his bed, propped up against two pillows. Above
his head is a new poster of Bobby Fischer and Boris Spassky,
playing for the 1972 world chess championship. Fischer won
that match and donated $60,000, a third of his winnings,
to the Worldwide Church of God, which went a long way
toward solidifying him as Timmy's idol. But Fischer was
upset by the failed end-time prophecies, especially the one
in 1975. He's since quit the church and called Mr. Armstrong
a satanic madman plotting to rule the world. Now Timmy
idolizes Fischer even more.

"So," he asks when I hand him the paperback, "what do
you think?"

"I think I shouldn't have read that."

"Of course you should have," he says. "You don't want to be no sucker, do you?"

The old Timmy wouldn't have used the word *sucker*. Or double negatives. "No," I reply, "I don't want to be no sucker."

"Or no *vic*?"

Vic: an abbreviation of *victim*. I recognize it from the book he gave me. The author is Robert Beck, though on the streets, when he was a pimp, he was known as Iceberg Slim. I guess now I'm learning how to speak like a pimp instead of an apostle. "I don't want to be no vic either," I tell him.

"Hell no, you don't."

I've never heard him curse before. He's taking my scholarship to the next level, but I'm not ready to join him up there, so I just shake my head.

"Hell no," he says again. "*Shit.*"

I shake my head more vigorously.

He gets two more books from beneath his bed. These are by Donald Goines, another ex-pimp, I know, because I already read the jackets while going through Timmy's things. Donald Goines's life was cut short at age thirty-eight by multiple gunshots to the head. Iceberg Slim got his nickname for continuing to sip his cocktail after a stray bullet pierced his fedora. I don't know what this study is preparing me for, but I'm worried.

Bubba is also being prepared for something, but I don't know what his is either. I'd ask him, but he doesn't speak to me anymore, other than to correct me when I call him Bubba because he wants to go by Jimmy now. My mother says he doesn't like speaking, because he's self-conscious about his stuttering. Maybe that's true in general, but it seems to be more than that with me. I think he's upset that

I was invited to Whitney Young and he wasn't. Ever since I told him about it, he's spent most of his time with Timmy, who, instead of giving him books, takes him for long drives in our station wagon or hangs out with him in our garage. They're in the garage now. I'm standing at the door, trying to get in, but it's locked. I knock and say it's me.

Bubba tells me to go away.

"Why?"

"B-b-b-b-b-cau-cau-cause," he responds, "you're a-a-a-a vic!"

There's laughter before Timmy opens the door, closing it quickly behind himself after he steps outside. He cups his hands around his lips and blows off the May evening chill. "Hey, Jerry. What's up?"

"Can I come in?"

"No," he says. "Not yet. But soon."

"Why not?"

"Soon," he repeats. "Hey, did you finish those books I gave you?"

I have. He says he'll give me some more. I don't want any more. The violent plots are affecting my dreams, sometimes to the point where I wake with a jolt and pounding heart, believing I've just committed or been the victim of assault or murder. I want to read something light, preferably funny, which I guess is how his conversations go with Bubba, since when they're over all either of them can do is grin and giggle. It doesn't occur to me, and it wouldn't have in a million years, that their joviality is the result of smoking marijuana.

Of course, I know the drug can make you jovial; our ministers concede as much during their regular sermons against its usage. Mr. Armstrong has as well in his booklet

New Facts about Marijuana, published in 1970 and soon afterward a likely staple in every Co-Worker's home, especially the ones with teenagers. Jovial, dreamy, lethargic, and pleasantly hallucinogenic—these are the rewards of the elusive good trip. But the bad trips, which are much more common especially among people who have what Mr. Armstrong calls "poorly organized personalities" (and people with poorly organized personalities, he notes, are the very ones who would want to smoke pot in the first place), can destroy your life. Bad trips result in rapes, psychosis, paranoia, heroin addiction, and retarded offspring. They lead to immorality and criminal behavior. They make you a *heathen* with a capital *H*. "What kind of a trip will you have?" is the question all would-be pot users have to ask themselves, and the answer can be found only by taking a roll of Satan's dice. I roll them in June.

Timmy has brought me to the garage. As soon as I open the door, Bubba welcomes me in with a cold can of Schlitz. He has one too. Timmy has a joint. He puts it between his lips and strikes a match. "This," he says from behind the flame, "is what's known as Moroccan Gold." He takes a slow drag, and after a pause the smoke seeps from his nose and rolls up his face. He hands the joint to Bubba, who performs the same move with aplomb. I didn't realize how much I wanted their company and acceptance until Bubba asks if I want to try a hit, and I say yes. He passes me the joint and tells me to hold the smoke in my lungs before exhaling it through my nose." I fail. Somewhere between my throat and nasal passage the smoke explodes. But I take advantage of a thirty-second coughing fit to rationalize the situation, telling myself that this is *hedonism* with a small *h*, because

I'll never do it again. While I'm doubled over making this promise to myself and God, Timmy takes the joint from me. The joint soon comes back, and even though there's another explosion, it's smaller and doesn't make me cough. By the third time around the explosions are gone. And then the joint is too. I don't feel anything, other than nervous expectation. While I wait to see what kind of a trip I'll have, I listen to Timmy criticize the church.

I'm not comfortable with his criticism. I understand that he's struggling with his faith, but I don't know what he's basing his opinions on, other than the delayed end-time prophecies. But at the moment it doesn't matter. All that matters is that I've finally been allowed to join them in the garage, and I want to show my gratitude by being attentive to his blasphemy and smoking his marijuana.

When we finish we go inside the house to watch TV. *Mork & Mindy* is on. I have seen a few episodes before and thought it was dumb, but I was wrong. The humor is first-rate. My brothers and I enjoy some good laughs for a while, then empty the kitchen of all the snacks we can carry. Before long Bubba dozes off on the couch. I want to doze off as well, but Timmy starts up again about the church. This time, instead of simply listening, I ask him what's caused him to feel this way.

"A lot of things," he says.

"The failed prophecies?"

"Yeah. But there's also some stuff you don't even know about."

"So how do *you* know about it?"

"Let's just say," he responds, "that the truth has been *revealed* to me."

Maybe his use of the phrase *revealed to me* is coincidental, and he doesn't intend to sound like the very man he's trying to turn me against. But he does sound like him, and this sticks with me for the rest of the night and into the following week, when I bring it to his attention.

The pusher is loitering in front of a liquor store when Timmy pulls to the curb. Their transaction is swift, done with an economy of words and motion: ten seconds after we double-park, the man has Timmy's money and Timmy has the man's dope.

We make a U-turn and park a half block away in the lot of a funeral home, the car positioned in such a way that the bustle of Seventy-ninth Street is our theater. I can still see our pusher working his area of the stage. He walks alongside someone for a while, usually a teenaged male, and then walks with another teenaged male going the opposite direction. Sometimes they pause and a deal is made. When a cruiser approaches, the pusher ducks into one of the doorways between the stores that lead to apartments overhead.

I turn to Timmy. "Hey," I begin, "remember last week, when you said things about the church had been revealed to you?"

He nods.

"You sounded like Mr. Armstrong, you know. He's always saying God *revealed* things to him."

"And?"

"And, you're saying *God* revealed things to you?"

"Absolutely."

"God? God spoke to you?"

"Yes." He runs his index finger and thumb over his lips and down his chin, tracing the route of his horseshoe mustache. "And do you know what he said was easier to do than get the truth out of Mr. Armstrong?"

"What?"

"To make a watch while wearing boxing gloves." He smiles and adds, "That's a direct quote."

It is a direct quote, but not God's. It's Iceberg Slim's. Or Donald Goines's. I can't remember which pimp, but I know the phrase came from one of the books Timmy gave me. I bring up those books now, saying I didn't really like them and don't want to read any more. He tells me it's important that I do.

"Why?"

"So you'll be prepared."

"For what?"

"The end."

"Of the world?"

"No," he says. "The South Side."

There's no denying that things are getting worse. A few weeks after I was robbed, it happened to my father. He was less than a block from our house when two men attacked him; one putting him in a bear hug while the other rummaged through his pockets, taking his wallet along with his watch, even though the numbers beneath the liftable glass face were in Braille. The next day he went to work as if nothing had happened, armed with his briefcase, cane, and faith in God's protection and in full denial that the neighborhood has changed. The white flight he and my mother were concerned about long ago ran its course, the sole holdout on our block an old man named Mr. Griffin, who sits in his second-story window preemptively ordering kids off of his lawn. Many of the mom-and-pop businesses that abruptly closed are now liquor stores and taverns. Some businesses are still empty. Pushers, like the one from whom Timmy made his score, seem to be everywhere. "Mark my words," Timmy says, "it won't be much longer before this whole area is worse than the West Side ghetto we left."

"And the books," I ask, "are to prepare me for this?"

He tears off two sheets of rolling paper from the packet and licks one before affixing it to the other. Then he folds them, making a crease where he begins sprinkling on the buds. "Remember, if you put in too much, it won't close properly and the joint might even split. Too little, and you're inhaling mostly paper. It's got to be the right amount." After he's sprinkled on the right amount he rolls the paper around the marijuana, pausing to lick the last quarter inch before making the seal. He hands me the book of rolling papers and the bag of marijuana. I tear off two sheets of paper and get started. "And you know what else?" he says. "There'll be *serious* drugs being dealt, not just weed. Weed is nothing. I'm talking speed, cocaine, heroin. And when *that* happens . . ." His voice trails off. My imagination takes it from there.

"And the books," I say, "are a preview of this future?"

He gestures toward the joint I'm making. "Crumble the buds more thoroughly."

I pinch off a large bud and crumble it over the folded paper. He nods approvingly.

"So the books," I continue, "are like a preview, a warning?"

"Not a warning. A blueprint. They'll teach you how to protect yourself against thieves and hustlers, like the Armstrongs."

I've finished making my joint. I've put too much in the middle and not enough in the ends. It looks like a piece of hard candy. I sit it in the ashtray. Timmy's is as perfect as a pencil. He lights it and offers it to me, but even though I had a good trip the first time, I stick to my promise and refuse. As I listen to him try to convince me of pot's harmlessness, I watch pedestrians move about in the scorching midday sun. There are a fair number of children in swimsuits carrying towels, obviously heading to and from the beach. Men drift in and out of the taverns. Women walk by carrying grocery bags and steering strollers. I imagine them all being heroin dealers and prostitutes as I dart around them, navigating their dangerous solicitations until I reach Baskin-Robbins 31 Flavors, the Place of Safety.

"What's so funny?"

I stop chuckling to say, "The Place of Safety."

He chuckles too, but for a different reason. "How stupid did we have to be to believe that?" he asks, and I say very stupid, but the truth is that I still do. I still believe Mr. Armstrong is God's apostle. I still believe in the seven holy days, that it's wrong to celebrate Christmas and birthdays, and that the moment of Christ's return can be counted in days, maybe hours. I especially believe in the lake of fire, and I see myself in it every time Rachael lets me fondle her, as she did, most recently, this morning. I still believe all the teachings of the church, not because I want to but because I don't know how to stop. Instead of merely filling my brain, the doctrines give it its shape, like a cookie cutter pressed into dough.

"How do you unbelieve a belief?" I ask.

"In what? The Place of Safety?"

"In anything."

"Easy. Replace it with another belief, preferably one that's true."

"How do you know what's true?"

"You have faith," he says.

Last week he sounded like Mr. Armstrong. Now he sounds like our parents. "It's that simple? Just have faith?"

"Have faith," he continues, "in fact not theory. Faith in things you can see, things you can measure. In mathematics there's a term called a *demonstrable proof.* It means no matter how many times you test for something, the result will always be the same. Put your faith in these kinds of results."

"So what's your demonstrable proof that Mr. Armstrong isn't the true messenger?"

"Wrong question. You should be asking, What's the demonstrable proof that he is."

His joint is nearly finished. I decline again when he offers it to me. "Then what's your demonstrable proof that he's a crook and a liar?"

He glances around, I assume to check for the police, and it occurs to me that if they catch us, I could be in serious trouble, even though I'm not getting high. I tell him I'm ready to leave. He ignores me and says, "Mr. Armstrong gives a date for the end-time, and we send him money to help spread the word that the Tribulation is coming. The Tribulation doesn't come. What does he do? Changes the date, or denies he ever set one. What do the Co-Workers do? Send him more money. When the new date is wrong, he changes the date again, and then he denies he set it again. He's sent more money. Same test, same result. It's a shell game, an elaborate con that's making him richer and richer and his followers poorer and poorer. He's the best con man there is. And you know what that makes the Co-Workers?"

"Marks and tricks?"

"Wrong again."

"Vics?"

"Hypocrites."

"Hypocrites?"

He turns the ignition. "Matthew 24," he says, as the engine explodes to life. *"But if that wicked servant tells himself my master is delayed, he will be stabbed and put with the hypocrites."*

I stare at him, confused, and before his face breaks and the car rings with his wild laughter, I wonder if the old Timmy has returned, if I'm witnessing a spontaneous rebirth of his faith. I wonder, and I hope.

The phone rings. It's a prostitute. She's calling to say she needs to see a doctor because she has "female problems." They will cost $400 to treat. Earl the Black Pearl consents to the expense and hangs up, and as some other pimps begin teasing him for spending that kind of money on a whore, Timmy comes into my room and takes the book from my hands. He replaces it with Mr. Armstrong's most recent newsletter, dated June 28. 1978. *Dear Brethren of God's Church and Co-Workers with Christ,* it begins. *This is the most difficult letter I have ever been called on to write. I would give my left arm rather than write it if that could nullify what Satan has done to make this letter necessary.*

I pause and look up. "What's this about?"

"Read on," Timmy says, lowering himself onto the beanbag chair next to my bed. "Read on."

I read on. The letter resumes with this reminder: God used him, Mr. Armstrong, as the only apostle of our time to start the church in 1933. Ambassador College opened fourteen years later with the sole mission of training ministers for The Work. The first few years of the church were tough going, because Satan sought to destroy it at every turn, mainly through the secular faculty, the only kind available at the time, who tried to put God on the periphery of the curriculum or remove him altogether. Mr. Armstrong would have none of that, however, and things were made right, even though it took him another fourteen years.

By then Garner Ted was eighteen. Without his parents' knowledge or consent, he enlisted in the navy for a four-year tour of duty that ended in 1952. He enrolled in Ambassador College that fall, though he was less interested in what he referred to as "dad's religion" than in the office manager position he'd receive as a student. His conversion was uncertain, but by 1955, when Mr. Armstrong launched the televised version of his radio broadcast *The World Tomorrow*, Garner Ted had come to accept his father as the true apostle, and himself, should it be necessary, as his heir. Garner Ted was put in charge of the radio broadcast, and fourteen years later, in 1969, after he'd honed his evangelical skills, his father gave him the reins of the television show. The problems began there. His first disfellowship was in 1971. It was kept confidential, known only to Mr. Armstrong and a few high-ranking officials.

I didn't even realize disfellowships could be confidential. Even now Mr. Armstrong doesn't name Garner Ted's sins, but he does say that, after Garner Ted repented and was reinstated later in the year, excessive drinking and gambling resulted in him being disfellowshiped again. That disfellowshipment was also kept confidential. As was the next one in 1972, when the Co-Workers, waiting for the Great Tribulation, were told only that he was in the bonds of Satan.

I pause reading for a few seconds. It's too much to take in all at once. A thorough digestion will require much more time, but my uneasiness about the secrecy of the disfellowships, the sheer hypocrisy of it, is instant. I think of Mr. Martin, how he was humiliated, expelled, then sentenced to eternal death, while Garner Ted's reputation and church status went unblemished, his salvation, at least for the time being, secure. It doesn't help that Mr. Armstrong defends this secrecy by drawing a comparison between himself and Richard Nixon. Apparently the disgraced president's illegal actions had been in keeping with God's teachings, which tell us, Mr. Armstrong writes, that, "love covers." Nixon's cover-up arose out of his love for the country; Mr. Armstrong's cover-up arose out of his love for his son. Had Jesus been the president, Mr. Armstrong continues, he would have covered up Watergate too. And then Mr. Armstrong writes this: *I have only followed the WAY OF CHRIST, trying desperately through the years to COVER UP my son's sins and mistakes—while at the same time NOT condoning his sins, but trying to give God's kind of punishment which CORRECTS AND RESTORES to the grace of GOD, rather than act in hostility and revenge.*

The time for hostility and revenge has come. Garner Ted, according to his father, has been secretly conspiring with Satan to take over the church. The father's response: another disfellowship, the unforgiving kind with which the rest of us are familiar. *That means, brethren*, he writes, *that on pain of being themselves disfellowshiped and PUT OUT of God's Church, you are all, according to CHRIST's COMMAND, restrained from contact with, or conversations with, Garner Ted Armstrong—no longer a member of this Church!*

There's more. I don't read on. I sit the newsletter next to me on the bed and ask if our parents know.

"I just read it to them."

"What'd they say?"

"They're shocked, but, you know, also kind of not shocked. They've heard the rumors."

"What rumors?"

"About the drinking and gambling."

"When?"

"A while ago. A couple of years, at least."

"Who else knew?"

"Lots of people."

"You?"

He nods again.

"Tommy? Mary?"

"And Linda," he says. "And there've been other rumors. They were in that *Times* article."

The *Times* article was mentioned in the newsletter. It was called, "Garner Ted, Where Are You?" and published in 1972 after word of one of the disfellowships leaked to the press. Timmy tells me he read it. "Basically," he says, "it accused Garner Ted of a whole lot of womanizing and his father of a whole lot of hustling, ripping off his struggling brethren while he lives in style. The old man's a hustler, Jerry. Garner Ted is too. The church is half con, half cult. That's what I've been trying to tell you." He pauses, waiting for me to respond. When I don't, he rises and slowly walks across the room. But instead of leaving, as I thought he would, he pulls the door closed and faces me, and I understand something worse is coming. He's sensed my vulnerability and knows the time is ripe for the kill.

"Now that you're finally learning the truth," he says, "there're a few more things you may as well know."

"Like what?"

"Like Bill."

"Bill? Who's Bill?"

"You don't remember Bill?"

I shake my head.

"Do you remember Winkle?"

Winkle, Winkle, Winkle, our baby brother. It's been five years since his last visit, and as I try to picture his face, I only see mine. And so for the rest of my life, whenever I think of him, I will be the little boy with the man who, Timmy tells me, is his real father.

I stand and call him a liar. He moves toward me, his finger in my face as he orders me to sit down. When I don't, he threatens not to tell me more, and now I'm saying, "More? More?" but I stop when he grabs my arm and pulls me with him. First we go to his room, where he takes a brown paper bag out of his closet, and then we go to the garage, where the contents of the bag are unloaded: rum, coke, and two plastic cups, an emergency kit, of sorts, prepared specifically for this moment.

While we drink, he recounts our parents' history, how they married at age eighteen and had three kids in three years. A year later they added another. My father was in college at the time, studying to become a guidance counselor for people with disabilities, the kind of expert who could help you cope with the stresses that had driven him to booze. He drank heavily every night, rye and bourbon back then instead of beer, returning from the corner tavern at three, four in the morning with the help of one of the regulars, or sometimes a Good Samaritan would have discovered him wandering the streets, unable to find his way. On the nights he misplaced his keys he would bang on the door until our mother let him in, or, when she refused, until the police responded to a neighbor's call and took him to sleep off his excess in a cell. In the morning there would be apologies, prayer, and Bible study. When these ceased to appease my mother, she asked for a divorce, which was like asking for death, their minister told her, because that was

God's penalty for breaking the bond of marriage. But she felt dead already. She was ready to die again.

The minister convinced her to postpone the divorce but not a separation. In December of 1963, two months before Bubba and I were born, my father moved out. In his absence, my mother was courted for two years by Bill. He was thoughtful, intelligent, and kind, Timmy says, and yet a week after Bill placed a ring on my mother's finger, she removed it and reconciled with my father. But before he returned home, he had to agree to give up hard liquor, and my mother, after discovering she was pregnant, agreed to give Bill full custody of their son.

"Why'd she let Daddy back?" I ask.

Timmy takes a drink and follows it with a long pause. "Because she couldn't unbelieve a belief."

"In the church?"

"No," he says. "In him."

I finish my drink. Timmy makes me another one. I ask if anyone in the church knows who's Winkle's real father. "No one knows," he says. "Just the family. That's why they told everyone he died. Actually, they never said he died. They said they *lost* him. Which, technically speaking, was true."

But our mother told Bubba and me he was in heaven. I remember that. She told us he was resurrected and adopted . . . *by Bill*, the man I thought was Jesus. I actually thought *Jesus was in my home.* Yet for some reason this seems less absurd than Bill and my father being there together. I ask Timmy about this, and he says our mother wanted to hold Winkle one last time before we left for Petra, and at first Bill wouldn't let Winkle come to our house alone. And then Bill threatened not to let him come at all, a threat he finally fulfilled. In the meantime other Winkles came, foster child after foster child, my mother's desperate attempt, I'll understand when I'm older, to resurrect her lost son. But for now I'm just a confused fourteen-year-old boy, getting drunk for the first time and hurting from the sting of a parent's lie.

The rum and cokes are finished. We're leaving the garage. Timmy is telling me I shouldn't dwell on the specifics of what he's said. Focus on the larger points, he's telling me, the important points, like how the world is full of deception, how very few people can really be trusted, how it's important that I learn to think and make decisions on my own. I'm trying to make sense of his advice, but my thoughts are spinning along with the ground. He has his arm around my shoulder, helping me walk, and I am my father now, stumbling home, struggling back to a life I can no longer handle. When we reach the door and find it locked, the anger that has been building in me surfaces. I bang on the glass. Timmy moves in front of me, tells me to take it easy. He digs into his pocket for his key. I throw a punch, aiming over his shoulder.

The lobby is a madhouse of crying babies and shouting drunks, seniors moaning on gurneys, teenagers clutching arms and wrists, men with bruised faces, vagabonds snoring in chairs and reeking of urine. After nearly an hour with them, I'm glad to be in my own room, though it's not so much a room as a space partitioned from other spaces by curtains. Behind the curtain on my left a man complains of sharp stomach pains. To my right a woman's having heroin withdrawal. In front of me is the nurses' station, and surrounding it more people behind more curtains, many of them suffering badly, like my neighbors and me.

The nurse assigned to end my suffering is named Ruby. She rolls a stool from beneath a small corner desk and sits on it, holding a clipboard and pen. She's around sixty years old, I guess, her red hair tinged with gray and framing a kind face, one not fully capable of looking stern, though she gives it a good effort by pursing her lips and squinting. "You'll need to tell me the truth," she says, "so I can get you the help you need."

"I am telling you the truth," I say. I told her what I told my father; I tripped and extended my hand to break my fall. Like my father, the nurse asked why I would try to break my fall with my knuckles. Unlike my father, who'd had a few drinks himself and didn't press me, the nurse asked if I was intoxicated. I confessed to having a glass of wine with dinner, describing it as a religious custom. She asked if I had trouble with anger. That was when Timmy, who so far had stood quietly by the center curtain, said we were God-fearing Christians who live our lives with humility, gentleness, and patience, as prescribed in the book of Ephesians. Ruby sent him back to the lobby.

Now she writes something on her clipboard, pausing to admonish me to keep my hand a little higher. I raise it level with my chest, the bloody bandage—one of my white tube socks—just beneath my chin. When Ruby peeked under the sock a little while ago the bleeding had stopped and my ravaged knuckles were visible, as well as the specks of glass embedded in my flesh, glinting like gold dust.

Ruby rests her clipboard on her lap. "Let me put it this way," she says. "If you don't tell me the truth, I'll have to assign you to a case worker. And maybe involve the police."

I think this over and make a proposition. "I'll tell you the truth, if you don't assign me to anyone. I just want to go home."

"We'll see. I can't promise you anything. How'd it happen?"

I hang my head, like a person full of contrition. "I punched out a window," I mumble, "on a dare."

"A dare?"

I nod. "Just to prove that I could do it. It was stupid, *I* was stupid."

She doesn't say anything immediately, which I take to mean she's willing to be convinced. I only have to offer up more details. I draw them from the same place I drew the dare: a scene I read in a novel where some teenaged delinquents stole a bottle of whiskey from one of their parents' bars and drank it at an abandoned warehouse. They tossed rocks at the windows for a while, and then one kid challenged another to show his manhood by punching out a glass pane. I switch the warehouse to a synagogue, though, since there is an abandoned one not far from my house. And I explain that the window had wire mesh, which wasn't the case in the novel, nor was it the case in the window on our back door. It has newly installed burglar bars.

"How often do you drink with your friends?"

"This was my first time."

"Tell me the truth."

"I am, I am. Before tonight the only alcohol I'd ever had, like I said, was wine with dinner." I glance up, locking my eyes with hers, which are asking me for a little more. "Manischewitz," I tell her. "Concord Grape."

She writes something on her clipboard. "Have you learned your lesson?"

"Yes," I say. "I swear to God."

"No need to do that," she responds. "I believe you."

The third commandment; I recited it once for the deacons. The words began to fill my brain, as if pumped there from a syringe, and I'm smiling as I relay them to Ruby. "'Thou shalt not take the name of the Lord God in vain, for the Lord will not hold him guiltless that taketh His name in vain.'"

Ruby's squinting again. "Do you and your brother reference the Bible often?"

"Yes," I say, grinning. "We're the Chosen Ones."

"Very funny." She has me follow her to the sink, where she removes the sock. The blood is dry and matted to the wound. She rinses it off with cold water. Then she drenches my hand in iodine, as I once imagined Paul drenching his boils.

"Can you wiggle your fingers for me?"

I wiggle my fingers. Fresh blood seeps through the cuts.

"Okay," she says. "Good. No broken bones, but you'll probably need a few stitches. How's your pain?"

I felt none until now, which I guess means I'm sobering up. "It hurts a little."

"It should hurt *a lot*. Go have a seat. I'll be right back."

She isn't right back. I wait at least another hour. I assume the purpose of the delay is to have me reflect on my reason for being here and evoke deep regret. It does. Only instead of reflecting on my alcohol consumption and subsequent loss of temper, I take a broader view of the matter. I'm here because I don't know who or what to believe anymore. I don't regret punching out the window. I regret being born.

Ruby pushes through the curtain with a medical cart, followed by a woman who introduces herself as Dr. McCracken. She's young and pretty, and I know this has a purpose too; to make me feel awkward and stupid, especially when she says, "I hope you don't plan to fight any more synagogues."

"No, I don't," I say, returning her smile. "That was the first and last one."

"Good. Because you'd lose again."

She picks up a pair of latex gloves from the cart and works them onto her delicate-looking hands. After drawing my hand toward her she nods at my knuckles. "You definitely need stitches," she says. "I see you've had some before." She's looking at my scar. "How'd that happen?"

"A dog bit me. My friend's dog."

She takes the tweezers and pinches a sliver of glass from my flesh, wiping it on a square of gauze. "Were you teasing it?"

"No."

She digs out another piece of glass. "I won't be able to get all of these, but that's okay. They'll work themselves free over the next few weeks. Just pull them out once they protrude from the skin."

Glass protruding from my skin for the next few weeks? My life, I think, is becoming a real horror show.

"What were you doing?" asks the doctor.

"I accepted a dare."

"No, not the window. I mean when the dog bit you."

I tell her I was petting it.

"That's all? Nothing to provoke it?"

Paul thought so. He said I was trying to steal Milo's turkey bone, at least from Milo's point of view, but I explained that Milo was merely following God's command to punish me for celebrating Christmas. Paul saw the logic of this, pointing out that *dog* spelled backwards is *God*, something we'll joke about, off and on, for the next several years.

The doctor asks, "How old were you when it happened?"

"I was six."

"Only six? That's awful." She shakes her head in sympathy.

I join her. My life isn't becoming a real horror show, I'm thinking. It's been one for a long time.

If a man has a stubborn and rebellious son, who will not obey the voice of his father or the voice of his mother, and, though they discipline him, will not listen to them, then his father and his mother shall take hold of him and bring him out to the elders of his city at the gate of the place where he lives, and he shall say to the elders of his city, "This our son is stubborn and rebellious; he will not obey our voice, he is a glutton and a drunkard." Then all the men of the city shall stone him to death with stones. So you shall purge the evil from your midst, and all Israel shall hear, and fear. (Deuteronomy 21:18–21)

Our father must have heard, and feared. It's three months after our minister read this scripture, delivered on the heels of Garner Ted's disfellowship as a rebuke of his actions, and our father cites it before throwing Tommy out of the house.

But the scripture does not apply. Tommy is nothing if not obedient, disciplined, moderate, and sober. While a sophomore in high school he started working as a bagger at the corner grocery store; at eighteen he enrolled in a technical college to study computer programming; at nineteen he was hired as a technician at a bank; by twenty he was Mr. Armstrong's staunchest supporter, ready to criticize anyone whose lifestyle contradicted church teachings. His only vice, as far as I can tell, is his militancy against vices.

And so rather than citing that passage from Deuteronomy, our father should have cited the one from Psalms warning against wrath, or the one from Romans that warns against passing judgment, or the one from Proverbs that assures us no one's heart is pure, although, while Tommy was beating Bubba, what crossed my mind was the line from Exodus exhorting us not to kill.

Before their fight started, Bubba and I were in the basement playing pool. I had just watched him pump his stick between his fingers before darting it forward, hitting the cue ball flush and sending it careening across the table. The fifteen balls scattered on impact, but none found a pocket. "*D . . . d . . . damn,*" he muttered, shaking his head and backing away. I laughed and assessed my options. The best one was the six ball teetering over the right side pocket. I leaned against the table and took aim, concentrating too hard to hear the basement door open, the footfall on the stairs. I shot. The six ball dropped into the hole as I heard the word *sinners.*

I whirled around. Tommy was right behind me at the bottom of the stairs, holding his Bible and looking crazed. "I saw what you were doing in the garage," he said.

Bubba moved toward us from the other side of table. "You didn't . . . didn't . . . didn't . . . see . . . see anything."

"I saw you—."

"Shut . . . shut *up.*"

Tommy's eyes widened before he charged forward, punching Bubba on the chin and knocking him against the wall.

Bubba was back at him in a flash, swinging with a wildness that Tommy exceeded. Somehow they grabbed hold of each other and careened into the television, knocking it from its stand and onto the tile floor. The sound of the screen disintegrating into a million pieces was terrific, and soon my father rushed downstairs, asking what was going on, moving toward my screaming brothers with outstretched arms. He located them near the bathroom door, and I was there too, struggling to separate them, which now became possible with my father's help. He had a hold of Tommy; I had Bubba. Linda and our mother were at the top of the stairs.

Tommy explained through heaves that he saw Bubba and me smoking pot and drinking beer. We vehemently denied it. And so it was our word against his, leaving one indisputable fact: a twenty-one-year-old man raised a hand against his fourteen-year-old brother, grounds for his eviction. Within the hour he was gone, purged from our midst, and Bubba and I were back in the garage, where we remain, reestablishing our highs.

Timmy joins us. He was on a drug run when the fight started and now he's emptying an ounce of marijuana from a zip-lock bag onto the hood of the car. He's been selling it for the last two months, a part-time occupation that will become full time when he's caught with the drug at his work-study job as an accountant. His employer will fire him, his college will expel him, and then our father will purge him too. But this is four months off, all the way in February, and I can no more anticipate these events than I could have anticipated what happened to Tommy. Our father throwing him out simply doesn't make sense to me. Tommy's attack on Bubba doesn't either, though Timmy tries to explain it. "He was only trying to look out for you," he says. He licks the rolling paper and completes the seal of a joint before tossing it into a pile with a few others. "He was trying to look out for you, but he doesn't understand what's happening in these streets. *I* do. I'll look out for you now."

W
ith Tommy gone, the responsibility of driving us to and from church falls to Timmy. When we get into the car, especially when the weather turns cold, it reeks of the apple-scented incense he uses to mask the smell of pot. He always gets high before church. Sometimes Bubba joins him. I did a few times, but the drug made me so paranoid that once, when the minister read a scripture about God's disembodied hand, I saw it reaching through the ceiling to grab me. I had a bad trip. And so on those Saturday mornings when my brothers circle the block smoking a joint, I treat myself to some of Timmy's liquor. I never have a bad trip with liquor. It helps me not care about anything. Not caring about anything has been important to me for six months, since I learned the truth about the church and my half-brother.

This morning I had a shot of Crown Royal. So when the minister announces that several former church officials, with the backing of California's attorney general, have filed a lawsuit against Mr. Armstrong, accusing him of siphoning off church funds and tax evasion, I don't care if anyone hears me laugh. Maybe no one does anyway; the news has thrown the congregation into chaos, a cacophony of gasps and chatter that seem to so flummox the minister that all he can do is stare around the room, as if unsure of what to say or do. I look over my shoulder for Timmy. The seat he was in is empty. Bubba, sitting to my left and stoned, is grinning and shaking his head. Linda was covertly reading a novel and now she looks around confused. Across the room, I see Tommy lean toward his girlfriend and speak in her ear. He doesn't look in our direction. He hasn't acknowledged us since our father threw him out.

"Let us pray," the minister says at last. "Let us pray that the men behind these false charges be *exposed* as heretics and enemies of the Lord."

Mr. Armstrong does his part. For the last six months, he used the Co-Worker letters to criticize Garner Ted, especially his decision to launch a rival church, the Church of God International, but now a large part of the newsletters becomes a platform to rail against his accusers. He uses it to provide a new mailing address for tithes and special offerings too, lest the money—God's money, he calls it—ends up in the hands of the court-appointed receiver. He also takes time in the newsletters to justify his expenditures, the fine clothes and jewelry expected to adorn someone meeting heads of state and royalty; how he, as our representative and God's apostle, needs to stay at the best hotels; how the Steuben crystal he routinely gives as gifts to kings, emperors, and prime ministers is in keeping with the gifts Christ received as an infant. Mr. Armstrong has done nothing wrong, he insists, other than serve the Lord, for which he is being persecuted, as Jesus was persecuted prior to his crucifixion. But this should not come to us as a surprise. It is merely more evidence, Mr. Armstrong observes, that the end-time prophecies are being fulfilled.

In April 1979, *60 Minutes* picks up the story of the lawsuit. I watch it alone in my bedroom on a small black-and-white television, though I'm tempted to turn it off when Mike Wallace describes the church as a cult whose one hundred thousand members contribute $80 million a year, more than the revenues of Billy Graham and Oral Roberts combined. But I keep watching and take the grand tour of the church's sprawling headquarters in Pasadena, California, including Ambassador College, estimated to be worth over $150 million. Mike Wallace speaks of Mr. Armstrong's many homes, his chauffeurs and butlers, his priceless art and private jets, and he even interviews his son Garner Ted, who says, for the benefit of people who are still on the fence, like my parents, that his father is not God's true apostle. *That's it*, I think when the program ends. *Mike Wallace has put a knife into Mr. Armstrong's heart.*

It'll be removed in two years. The lawsuit will be dismissed, thanks to a change in California law, lobbied for by Mr. Armstrong's lawyers, that limits the state attorney's ability to investigate religious institutions. But until then, Mr. Armstrong makes the most of the notoriety. The day after the *60 Minutes* episode, he rushes out a newsletter saying, *And NOW the top-rated, most listened-to program on television, 60 Minutes, takes a below-the-belt swat at the Church and Work of the living GOD !* This work is expensive to perform, Mr. Armstrong explains. He is proclaiming the gospel, after all, by television, print, and radio. And then there is his personal evangelism, which requires him to travel the world. As proof he lists his itinerary: Australia, Ghana, Liberia, Kenya, India, Japan, Thailand, Holland, South Africa, Jamaica, the Bahamas, the Philippines, Costa Rica, and many other countries in Europe, Asia, Africa, and South America. He concludes the newsletter in usual form:

> Brethren, we need right now to TAKE ADVANTAGE of this tremendous publicity, and run FULL PAGE ads in many metropolitan newspapers, in TIME, in NEWS-WEEK, in TV Guide (double pages or 4-page inserts there), and also Reader's Digest, beside such overseas publications as Der Spiegel in Germany, and others. But the truth is, we do not have the money—such full page ads cost a lot of money—but produce a MASSIVE IMPACT—on many MILLIONS of people!

He reminds us of where the money should be sent. He stresses that it should be sent quickly.

My parents don't send any. In a month, when they finally get off the fence, it's to leave the church. Then, after only three weeks, they reconsider and resume attending services. They don't tell us the reason why. But I know what it is. They want their sight. The best hope for this, the only hope for it, in their view, is in continuing to believe in the church. So I can't blame them for their decision. And when I tell them I'm not going back, they can't blame me for mine. Because I want my sight too.

Moonlight shines through the basement window and illuminates our bodies entwined on my bed, where we've spent much of the last hour kissing. Kissing is the most we've done during the two months we've dated, but now, when I make my usual play for her breasts, she doesn't stop me. Surprised and eager to see where this development will lead, I lower my hand after a few seconds to her inner thigh. She pulls it away. "Don't," she whispers.

Her name is Joyce. When she moved to the neighborhood six months ago she was considered exotic for having a white father and a black mother, and for attending St. Thomas Aquinas, the Catholic high school for girls a mile away. I didn't know any Catholics, to my knowledge, and I understood very little about Catholicism, other than that, according to church teachings, it's identified in the book of Revelation as the Great Whore. The pope is the Scarlet Beast.

Joyce isn't aware of these teachings. None of my friends is except for Paul, and either he's forgotten them or is kind enough to pretend to have done so. Because the turnover of families in the neighborhood has been so complete, the only religious practice that raised eyebrows was that I attended church on Saturday. When questioned about this, I nonchalantly mentioned that Jehovah's Witnesses attend church on

Saturday, implying that that was my faith. For some reason this didn't evoke the scorn it had before.

I push myself onto an elbow to see the clock on the dresser. 12:13 a.m. When I rest back next to Joyce, she asks if I'm upset. I am, but I tell her no.

"I'm sorry," she says.

"It's fine. It's getting pretty late, though. We should get some sleep."

She nods before pulling me close to her. We kiss some more. She leans away after a while and whispers, "Do you want to?"

"Of course I do."

"You wouldn't tell your friends, would you?"

I already have. It's probably the most convincing lie I've ever told, since many of my friends have seen her sneak into my house for sleepovers, unaware that the only clothing we remove during the night, at her insistence, are our socks and shoes. "I would never tell a soul," I say.

"Not even Paul?"

I shake my head.

"You promise?"

I promise.

She says she believes me, but that she isn't ready. Then she lowers her hand to *my* inner thigh, lets it linger for several seconds before she rolls away, facing the wall. Over her shoulder, she says there's something she has to tell me.

"What?" I ask, and suddenly I know. I bolt upright. "You've already fornicated."

"*Fornicated?*" She faces me again. "Who says that?"

"With Paul, wasn't it?"

"Seriously. You need to update your slang by, like, two thousand years."

"That's why you don't want me to tell him."

"No, you *jerk*. I didn't *fornicate* with your dumb friend!"

"Then what do you have to tell me that's so bad?"

"Who said anything about it being bad? Maybe it's good."

"So *what* is it?"

She rolls over again. "It's very personal. And confusing."

"Okay . . ."

"You really want to know?"

I do, I say, and a year later, when she finally tells me the truth, I'll replay this conversation and see so clearly that she was trying to come out to me. She was struggling with her sexual identity, conflicted about her desires and her faith, conflicted about her feelings for me and a junior tennis star at her school—all this, for now, concealed in a single declaration: "I'm Catholic."

"That's it? That's all you wanted to tell me?"

"Yes."

"I already knew that."

"You don't understand. I'm *Catholic* Catholic."

I still don't understand. "Is that bad?"

"Maybe. Sometimes."

"Yeah, well. Try being a Chosen One."

"A what?"

"A Chosen One."

"Are you talking about being a Jehovah's Witness?"

"I'm not a Jehovah's Witness."

"Really? I could have sworn you said—."

"I didn't."

"So what are you?"

"Nothing. But I used to belong to the Worldwide Church of God."

"The Worldwide . . ."

"Church of God."

"I've never heard of it."

"Most people haven't. It's a doomsday cult." It's the first time I have called it that. Hair rises on my arms.

"A *doomsday* cult? You mean, like those Jim Jones people?"

"No, no, not like that at all. A man named Herbert W. Armstrong started ours. He preached that the Great Tribulation would start in 1972, Christ would return in 1975, and that our church was God's only true church. All others were the devil's, especially Catholicism."

"That's insane," Joyce says.

"I know."

"That's beyond insane."

I agree.

"When did you leave this cult?"

"I stopped going to church four months ago, when *60 Minutes* did a story on it. But I'd stopped believing in it before then."

Movement above us, someone walking. I shush Joyce. Even in the poor light I can make out her widened eyes, her fear of being discovered. Her parents think she's staying at the house of a girlfriend. "It's just my father going to bathroom," I whisper. She nods. In the moments we are quiet, my thoughts return to Jonestown, to the news images of bodies scattered about in an open field, babies swaddled in their mothers' rigid arms, hundreds of lives discarded like so much debris.

I never made a connection between the Peoples Temple and the Worldwide Church of God. I should have. I can definitely imagine Mr. Armstrong ordering us to take our lives when the end-time prophecies failed. And we would have done it. Many of his followers still would, I am certain, including half my family. Mary and Tommy remain believers like my parents; Linda has doubts but continues to attend church, while Bubba, Timmy, and I think they're all fools. Religion, once so central to my family's identity, is no longer even a subject for family discussion. I miss it. I miss it because I understand that something greater than our collective faith has been lost. And it won't be regained. Not even after all of us have left the church, which will be in a few years, thanks to evidence surfacing that Mr. Armstrong committed incest with his daughter for a decade, beginning in 1933, when she was thirteen.

Footsteps again, then silence. When I'm certain the threat has passed, I ask Joyce about the Holy Trinity, which has never made sense to me before. It makes even less sense after she explains it. (*Three* spirit beings, but really only *one?*) Then she confuses me further by explaining the Eucharist and Communion. She tells me about what happens at Mass. She seems to enjoy talking about her faith, and so I let her, even though, after a while, I stop paying attention, because my ignorance is upsetting me. There's so much I don't know about other religions and beliefs, about anything, really. I don't even know how to be black.

For October the weather's unseasonably warm, probably in the high seventies. I've walked only a block from the train platform and I'm already perspiring in my old church suit. I remove my jacket and carry it over my shoulder as I walk the next block to Whitney Young High. I've always been curious to see the campus in person. Since it's not far out of my way, I figure this is as good a time as any.

The massive building is made of concrete and steel and spans an entire block. As I near the main entrance, the afternoon bell rings, sending out a wave of nerdy teenagers, and it's upsetting to know I should be among them. I understand that there was no devil's plan to harm me. There was only a twelve-year-old boy who was raised to think of death and one day found himself on the verge of life. There was fear.

Now there is regret. I experience it every time I enter South Shore High, where gangs are rampant, classes are too easy, bright students are teased and bullied. Pot is sold and smoked in bathroom stalls while craps are shot opposite the urinals. I barely made it through my first year. I already know I won't make it through my second.

I'm skipping a lot of classes. If I'm not at home pretending to be sick, I'm loitering in some park until the school day ends, or I take long walks, sometimes heading to the beach to watch men play chess on boards painted on cement tables. Timmy's often there. He's making good money off of his chess matches and better money from the pot he sells out of his old college book bag. I carry pot in my book bag too. I tried selling it at school, mainly in an effort to fit in, but thugs kept taking it from me, so now I sell it only to Paul and some of our friends. After we smoke it in my garage, we go to my bedroom to listen to Parliament Funkadelic while a strobe light makes us vanish and reappear.

But pot still is not my drug of choice, and so instead of getting high, I usually head to Seventy-ninth Street to stand outside a liquor store and petition passersby to help me make a purchase. If I misjudge someone, I risk getting a lecture or a scolding, and it's not uncommon for men to accept my money only to brush past me when they come out of the store, leaving me empty-handed. The drunks usually agree to help me without pause, though in exchange they'll want a couple of dollars or, worse, a swallow of my wine or beer. And so this is why, after finally saving enough money, I've come to the West Side to buy a fake ID. Only now, as I stand in front of Whitney Young, a part of me desperately wants to go inside to explain there's been a terrible mistake, that I'm the bright student the principal recruited in the seventh grade. "It's me," I mumble, as I turn to leave. "I'm the one . . ."

I cross the street and head south on Laflin Avenue. After turning left on Jackson Boulevard, I continue over the expressway and then make another left on Roosevelt Road. A right would send me to the Lighthouse for the Blind where, at this very moment, my father's hard at work, helping some unfortunate person come to terms with a loss of sight. When Bubba and I were toddlers, our father would take us to his office, but all I recall of those visits is crossing Roosevelt Road, where cars sped down the four lanes at fifty miles an hour. As soon as my father stepped off the curb, his cane raised high before him, like a lance, Bubba and I would wrap ourselves around his thighs. He'd yell for us to release him, and we'd yell our refusals, the prospect of being hit made all the more real by the screech of breaking tires. My first lesson in faith.

Two blocks later I reach the corner of Maxwell and Halsted. It's the western border of the open-air market known as Jew Town, where, for the last decade, the closest thing here to a Jew, I'd wager, is me. The Jews who immigrated here from Eastern Europe at the start of the century were replaced by the blacks who began arriving en masse from the South in the 1930s. I didn't know this history until recently, when Joyce explained it after I told her I was coming here. I didn't even know the name Jew Town refers to actual Jews, that it's a compound noun instead of a compound verb. I'd heard *jew* was synonymous with "to cheat," which is to say people went to Jew Town to be on the losing end of a financial transaction, unless they had their wits about them, in which case they could do well. I heard this from my cousins, the ones who used to tease us about not being black. I'm spending a lot of time with these cousins lately. They have their wits about them. They know things I need to know. They told me where to get the ID.

I remove the slip of paper from my pocket and reread the instructions: "White van, parked between a pile of old car tires and a polish sausage stand. Knock three times, pause, knock three more." I survey the area. There are a lot of polish sausage stands, and many piles of old tires. I do not see a white van. I see people, hundreds and hundreds of them, maybe thousands. I put away the paper and meander into the crowd. Maybe I can get a good deal on a bracelet for Joyce while I'm here.

I soon discover that if I walk too close to a store, someone near the entrance will take my arm and pull me inside. "You need one of these watches," they tell me, or these shoes, these scarves, these suits, these hats, and when I protest that I'm not interested, they wink and lower their price, waiting for me to recognize that I've outsmarted them, and then, when I continue to say no, they lower the price some more. Once I'm back on the street, men move toward me with gold necklaces dangling from their splayed fingers or show me sparkling watches that trail up their forearms. I decline their offers and keep walking, past the carts of fruit and ice cream stands, past the folding tables stacked with cassettes and eight tracks, past the bundles of boxer shorts, the lacy bras, the tube socks, and suede gloves, past the drug dealers who offer me discounts and the prostitutes who promise me bliss, past the musicians playing the blues near tins stuffed with dollar bills, and past the men who preach on corners waving Bibles, urging us to wake up, to save ourselves, while there's still time.

I buy a polish sausage. I've never eaten pork before; it's much saltier and greasier than beef, it seems, and after my second bite I start to feel queasy. I ball up what's left and head for a trashcan nearby, but as I reach it, a man blocks my path. He's wearing a navy three-piece suit and holding a leather briefcase that he asks me to watch while he finds a restroom. He extends the briefcase and smiles. I know this is some kind of a con; I read about similar ones in Timmy's novels. I step around him, throw away my sausage, and continue looking for the van.

It takes me thirty minutes but I find it. It's not near a polish sausage stand or a pile of tires. It's at the mouth of an alley by a used furniture store. The van's front windows are lowered; I hear music coming from inside as I approach. I knock on the door three times. I'm about to knock again when it opens. The person who answers looks to be a teenager himself, certainly no more than twenty. I expected someone much older and, given the space constraints, someone thin. He reminds me of the Fat Albert character from the Cosby Kids cartoon, only instead of a red sweater he wears a blue T-shirt, the sleeves squeezing his arms as if they were designed to cut off circulation. He scans the alley before waving me in.

He introduces himself as R.J. and motions toward a stool to my right. A white sheet hangs behind it, illuminated by a spotlight affixed from the rear of the ceiling. He sits on a stool across from me. Between us is a Polaroid camera on a tripod. "First things first," he says. "Sixty bucks." After kneeling to one knee, I take out four twenties, and I realize I've made a mistake when he asks if I want the standard ID or the deluxe one with an official state seal. I say the deluxe one. This costs me twenty more.

He hands me a card and pen to fill out my information. I write "Bobby Jenkins" as my name. For my year of birth I put 1959, which, in four months, would make me twenty-one instead of sixteen. I sign the card and give it back. R.J. sits it on the table to his left before leaning forward to the camera, pressing his eye against the viewfinder. I think to say *cheese* but decide against it seconds before the flash. When the image slides out, he takes it and swivels toward the table. He works quietly for several minutes before presenting me with the result.

My tie is crooked. My head is tilted a bit too much to the right. And my five o'clock shadow hasn't worked as well as I hoped. It looks a little like dirt, which it is, a thin layer I smeared across my upper lip where I have yet to even grow fuzz. I have no complaints about the craftsmanship, though. The ID looks good; it looks like the real thing. Just like that, I marvel, I'm someone else. But even before I climb out of the van, I realize this isn't true. I've been someone else for a while, ever since I quit the church. I'm someone with a future now, with my whole life ahead of me, and the choice of what to do with it is mine. I smile as the thought comes to me; I'm a god.

EPILOGUE

We stood inside the monastery, a sixty-five-foot structure carved directly into the mountainside. In contrast to its Hellenistic facade, complete with twelve ionic columns, the interior was simply one large open space. Our guide said it was likely a gathering hall for the Cult of Obadas, followers of the Nabatean king, or a tomb for his family. It was never used as a monastery. I whispered to my sons that it was never used as my bedroom either. They had a good laugh, as they did the first time I showed them photos of Petra and said I once thought this would be my home.

The single door didn't have stairs. To get inside we had to climb up five feet, a height from which I would have jumped if my knees hadn't been killing me. I winced as a teenager to our right ran forward and threw himself into the air. I squatted and slowly lowered myself over the edge before helping Brenda and the boys to the rocky plateau.

All around us tourists took pictures and congratulated each other for surviving the journey. Others rested up for the return trip on couches beneath a large tent. After we bought more water at a nearby concession stand, we found a cluster of seats near the tent's rear. Our guide joined us, as did the other members of our group; three administrators from the college where my wife worked as a vice president and their spouses. My wife and her colleagues had come to

Jordan to strengthen partnerships with two local schools. I had come to confront demons.

One of the spouses sat next to me and asked how I was doing. She knew about the cult. They all did. I'd mentioned it last night at dinner. They warned that the visit to Petra would be emotional for me, but they didn't know I used up that emotion long ago, often in ways that still made me cringe and wonder how I was alive. I had no emotions left, not as far as the cult was concerned. I'd come here to prove that to myself, and I believed I had; the trip felt like a vacation, no more or less stressful than any other. So I told the spouse I was doing fine. But I don't think she believed me. I lifted my bottle to my lips for a drink before realizing it was empty. I excused myself to buy more.

The concession stand line was long. While waiting I noticed people hiking up an adjacent mountain, its summit fifty yards above the monastery where a crowd of people stood looking around, some through binoculars, taking in what must have been a spectacular sight. The pain in my knees had subsided; I'd gotten my second wind. And so without another thought, I headed for the trail. But I didn't get very far. A minute in, I reached a sign with an arrow pointing the way. Its caption read "View the End of the World." And I could not bring myself to go on.

ACKNOWLEDGMENTS

Thank you to my agents Katherine Flynn and Ike Williams for their strong advocacy, and to my godsend editor, Helene Atwan, and all the fine people at Beacon Press for their keen insight and advice. For their thoughtful comments on various drafts, I am immensely indebted to Robert Atwan, Lundy Braun, Shaylin Hogan, Johnny Skoyles, and John Trimbur. My sons, Adrian and Dorian, deserve high praise for their smart feedback on the prologue and epilogue.

Completion of this book was aided by a special leave from Emerson College granted by President Lee Pelton, and with the encouragement of Maria Flook, Stephanie and Marc Rando, and Steve Yarbrough.

Finally, I am especially grateful to my wife and first reader, Brenda Molife, without whom this book specifically, and my happiness generally, would not exist.

9/16